Teaching Dance Beyond the Steps

A Guide For Dance Teachers Who Want To
Achieve Dance Teacher Mastery
And Become Industry Leaders

Jen Dalton

TEACHING DANCE BEYOND THE STEPS

TEACHING DANCE BEYOND THE STEPS

ISBN: 978-0-6486719-0-9 (pbk)
ISBN: 978-0-6486719-1-6 (ebk)

For more information about Jennifer Dalton or *Dance Teacher Central* head to: www.danceteachercentral.com or www.facebook.com/danceteachercentral/.

Typesetting and design by Publicious Book Publishing
www.publicious.com.au

Dedication

For Mia and Isla, who are the reason I do what I do.
Thank you for continually inspiring me to keep going and doing what I love!

Contents

Introduction

The art of teaching dance is as important as the art of learning dance.

I know you are passionate, creative and dedicated to making dance teaching your career. That's why you've picked up this book.

Times have changed. Things are different now. There is not only a new generation of students coming through the studio doors (and, with them, a new generation of dance mums), but also a new generation of dance teachers who dream big, who are inspiring, and who want to contribute more to this industry than just teaching dance.

I started teaching over 20 years ago. I have danced my way from the beginning as a student, through to assistant teaching and senior teaching, to ultimately becoming a studio owner. At the time of writing this book, I own six studios, manage a team of over 20 incredible teachers and staff, have over 1,000 students attend our classes each week, and run a highly successful teacher training program. But it didn't come fast and it wasn't particularly easy. I had to make the mistakes, work through the tears and frustrations, and learn along the way.

Your role as the next generation of dance teachers extends far beyond teaching the steps. You must connect, protect and educate like never before. You will make an impact in the lives of every single student who walks through your studio doors.

Over the years, I've discovered that becoming more aware of myself and others around me has been life-changing. I can't help but wonder if only I'd known the value and importance of this when I was younger and starting out, how I would have been able to save time and heartache to get to where I am now.

The mistakes that I've made along the way (which I absolutely don't regret) have enabled me to really think deeply and assess how students, teachers and parents have evolved in this industry ... and I love these changes. If we embrace not only some simple, practical ideas – such as planning and communication – but also understand the intangible ones – like awareness, connection and harnessing our creativity – the more we will flourish and create remarkable studios and cultivate beautiful learning environments to see our students thrive in.

It's all of this that drove and inspired me to sit down and write this book for you. I hope the information on the pages that follow encourages you to open your mind, absorb the lessons, gain a deeper understanding, and use this to develop a more empowered and exceptional teaching philosophy.

In a nutshell, the things I want you to know before we get started are:

1. Focus on your career as a whole – not just the destination, but also the journey to get there. I want you to see the big picture.

2. Do more than just motivate your students. Don't only show your students, but tell them *how* and *why* and share with them the positive impact they can have in this industry.

3. Remember this is a lifelong journey for you, personally. You will experience different seasons throughout your life. Some will be good, others not so good. But keep your head up, stay courageous, and be true to who you are and the difference you are making to those around you.

4. Change people for the better – don't just challenge them to change. Get your tutu dirty and get in there and show them how it's done!

5. Continue growing every day. Even if it's only a small step towards your goals, take action every single day. However, remember each goal is just one part of the whole journey.

So, it's time to forget what you think you know about dance education! There's a new generation of dance educators, and now is your chance to step up and make your mark.

I want to empower *you* to teach dance beyond the steps …

On a final note, the best way to work through this book is to have a notebook and your favourite pen (or the highlighting tool on your tablet device if you're reading it digitally) alongside you so that you can take notes and answer the questions I ask you throughout the chapters. I have also included helpful links with PDF downloads and resources, which I'd love you to keep copies of as they'll assist you in working through the book.

I hope you get as much value from reading it as I did from writing it, and that we will connect in the not-too-distant future.

Love in dance,

Jen x

Chapter 1
The Dance Teaching Evolution Process

When I stop and think about the great dance teachers and choreographers of the world – the true masters of our industry – the first three that come to mind are Mia Michaels, Galen Hooks and Fosse. They are each so different in their styles, strengths and approach, yet clearly they each possess something special that makes them stand out.

This got me thinking. What is it that an exceptional dance teacher has, or what have they done, to gain such a status? And is it possible for all of us to move through this same process and achieve greatness in our own right?

Each of these industry leaders has gone through type of 'apprenticeship': a time of observing, learning and practising. This is what took them from good to great, and gave them a platform to launch from to become an industry leader. They chose to think big and to have a voice – they are true leaders to us all. So the question is: Will you do the same?

I absolutely believe we all can transform from teacher to mentor and into an industry leader if we so desire. However, there is a process of evolution that has 4 stages, which we all need to go through in order to get there. This book is also going to take you through 5 principles you need to apply within each of the 4 levels of this evolution process, to show you exactly how to step into mastery and become an industry leader.

I've been teaching for many years now, continually growing, improving and challenging myself to get better and better. At the age of 12, while still dancing myself and finishing my syllabus and exam training, I started assisting my teacher at the studio I attended. My aunty owned the studio, so I was incredibly lucky to benefit from her guidance, mentoring and experience at such an early age. These days, assistant teaching opportunities are more readily available, but – back then – it was an honour to be asked and I took the role very seriously.

Over the years of assisting, I had opportunities to build solid relationships with the students and their parents, which eventually lead to the mother of one of the students asking if I could teach her daughter an extra class through the week to help improve her confidence. With the blessing and support of my aunty, I enthusiastically agreed. This was where my teaching journey started. I cleared out my parents' garage and off I went! Our first class was the following Tuesday. I was paid $3.00 for one hour! No business plan, no social media … no idea, really – just enough self-belief and passion that I wanted to share with others.

As a dance teacher – and in a role where I was clearly influencing the lives of the many students who walked into my classroom – my curiosity and desire to continue to grow, challenge and better myself led me to discover there is an evolution process that we move through as dance educators. This evolution is a 4-stage process. Regardless of which stage you are currently in in your teaching career – if you take the time and do the work, you can work through the stages, develop mastery in them, and become an industry leader.

Let me tell you about each stage:

The 4-Stage Evolution Model

Stage 1 of the Evolution Model: Student Teacher (or Assistant Teacher)

What you need to accomplish:
- Your technical training

- Experience as many different dance and performing styles as you can
- Observe as many difference teaching styles as you can
- Seek out opportunities to offer your time at your studio or company
- Strive for a great reputation from day one
- Know your true worth
- Open your mind and never stop learning

Stage 2 of the Evolution Model: Teacher

What you need to accomplish:
- Put your training into practice
- Connection with your students
- Learn to identify individual personalities within the class
- Planning and preparation
- Communication
- Trust and respect
- Keep your kids safe

Stage 3 of the Evolution Model: Mentor

What you need to accomplish:
- Develop leadership skills
- Train and guide other teachers
- Share your knowledge and experiences
- Give your time to other less experienced teachers
- Share more than your dance experience
- Nurture your students as well as younger teachers
- Embrace a wider personal approach

Stage 4 of the Evolution Model: Industry Leader

What you need to accomplish:
- Do your time
- Continue your own higher-level training

- Earn respect as an authority figure in the industry
- Know who you are and who you are not
- Adopt a mindset of giving, helping and making a change for the better

A significant side effect of being a teacher is that you will impact every student you come into contact with. This can be positive, negative or indifferent. You are ultimately in control of this and you must decide what type of impact you are going to have.

Teaching dance is not only about the steps, but the experience that will shape your students' future.

It can be the small, simple things you do or say that end up making a huge difference. These are learned during the different stages of your dance evolution education.

I'll now walk you through each step of each stage of the Evolution Model in more detail, so you don't miss anything.

Stage 1 of the Evolution Model: Student Teacher (Assistant Teacher)

The student teacher stage is where you need to start. This is your training stage.

Your Technical Training

You complete your technical training during the student stage, where you study dance through your dance studio, performing arts company or college, learning as much as you can about safe dance practice, technique and skills. Different studios will teach different syllabi. It doesn't matter which one you learn, as long as it covers the fundamentals and core foundations required for you to have a solid understanding of dance.

Have a conversation with your teacher or the principal and let them know about your desire to teach. Ask if there are any opportunities available for you to help out around the studio, assist alongside any of the senior teachers or observe other teachers while they are teaching, or help out at concerts and events. For many reasons, these types of opportunities are invaluable – but I'll go into it in more detail a bit later. Most importantly, use the time to make sure it is what you really want to do!

Experience as Many Different Dance and Performing Styles as You Can

I would encourage you to experience as many different dance and performing styles as you can. This will open your eyes to what you love to do and what you are really good at (as well as identify areas where you may be not as proficient). We all have genres that we are stronger in than others. This doesn't mean you can't teach all styles, but it's good to know where your strengths and weaknesses lie for you as a dancer.

When you step into mastery, when you reach that level, you can teach everything and everyone – but it helps to have a real passion and love for what and who you are teaching – so use this time wisely to help you gain clarity about where your focus lies.

Observe as Many Different Teaching Styles as You Can

Take the time to observe during your student teacher stage. Observe as many different teaching styles as you can. There are going be some teaching styles that resonate with you and some that won't. Take note of the type of impact the teacher is having. Is the teacher achieving student goals? Are the students progressing and improving? Is the teacher delivering with respect and are the students responding to the teacher with respect? It is here that I want you to look a layer deeper to see if the teacher is connecting with every one of the students in the class. Are the students listening? Are they responding? Are they engaged and wanting to give more? Observe what the teacher is doing, what they are saying (or what they are not doing or saying) and take note of their body language. This may give you some tips to try when it's your turn to get in front of a class.

Seek Out Opportunities to Offer Your Time at Your Studio or Company

As with any career, on the job training is the best experience anyone can get, so actively seek out opportunities to offer your time. Volunteer in any capacity at your studio, even if you aren't in the classroom straight away. Having the opportunity to experience as many different teaching styles, classroom management styles and events or production situations as possible is invaluable. This is the ultimate way for you to learn and grow exponentially and become really clear about where you are heading.

Strive for a Great Reputation From Day One

The dance and performing arts industry is small, so ensure you endeavour to prove yourself as a kind and decent human, and develop a positive reputation in the industry.

Your work ethic, your personality, your willingness to try, and your ability to think beyond what is expected of you, all start moulding you into the type of teacher you are going to be. You are a role model for many young people, and you are going to impact and shape them, so be conscious of everything you say and do.

Think about your attitude towards other people and how you respond in a group situation. Do you encourage negativity or gossip, or do you shut it down straight away? Do you thrive on drama and enjoy getting involved in everyone's business? If so, reconsider this type of behaviour. It will not serve you well once you step into your teaching role.

How do you behave on social media? What words and language do you use? What photos do you share? How does this reflect you and your personality? Ask yourself this question: 'If I was the parent of a young dancer, would I be happy with the content being shared on socials?' Start thinking about yourself as a role model and acknowledge that your actions need to reflect this. Essentially, give yourself every opportunity to work with and for the greats in the industry by developing an impeccable reputation from the very beginning of your career.

Know Your True Worth

Be realistic when you are first starting out. Our great teachers and leaders in the industry, who have decades of experience, have earned the right to name their price. A student coming from one or two years of study has not.

Once you finish your training and education and it's time to land your dream job, you need to be realistic about your pay rate. Generally, you should expect to be offered at or slightly above the award wage, as determined by Fair Work (Australia). If you are successful in your interview, most studio owners will give you a letter of offer of employment, which will include details about your rate of pay. I would not advise you to walk into the conversation and demand an outrageous hourly rate if you are just starting out. It certainly won't help you get the job!

I understand that money is essential in life. I know everyone needs to pay bills, eat and put fuel in the car. However, if at the beginning of your career you expect to make the same wage as someone in a 'normal' type of job, then you are mistaken. As with many creative jobs, you need to be driven by an element of passion and love in order for you to get through the first couple of years, but – trust me – if you put in the time and trust in the process, there is money to be made!

Open Your Mind and Never Stop Learning

Finally, in your student teacher stage, I want you to remember to open your mind and never stop learning, even after you land the job of your dreams.

Don't get complacent or fall into the belief that you know everything, because none of us ever do! If you do happen to start adopting this attitude, you'll find your career coming to a rather quick halt!

The dance industry is continually changing with new and exciting developments, teachings and opportunities, and we have a responsibility to our students to stay fresh and up-to-date with everything that is going on – this is part of the beauty of our industry.

As a side note, an exceptional teacher will consider themselves a student for life because they know and understand the importance of continuing to improve, grow, challenge themselves and never stop learning.

Once you have accomplished being a student teacher in Stage 1, and perhaps even landed your first paid teaching position, you can confidently move into Stage 2.

Stage 2 of the Evolution Model: Teacher

You have completed your technical training, you have assisted and observed as many different teachers and teaching styles as possible, and you've had experience as a student teacher in a whole range of dance styles. You may have even secured your first paid job, even if the pay is modest. You are 100 per cent confident that this career is for you and you feel the need and desire to be in a classroom to be able to share your passion and love of dance with others. This means you are exactly where you need to be to move into the next stage. The next stage is the teacher stage.

Put Your Training Into Practice

It is now time to put all that training and student teaching into practice. All the reading, practical training and learning you have done over the past several years now needs to be adapted and delivered by you, as the teacher, to your students. I want you to think back to your student teacher stage where you were assisting or observing different teachers. What resonated with you? What did you feel worked for others? What did you think was ineffective? When you're first starting out, you will learn to get a feel for your students and come to realise that what works for some, won't necessarily work for others.

Connection With Your Students

Now, I want to let you in on the secret of all secrets when it comes to being an exceptional dance teacher. It's about being able to truly connect with your students. Connection is the key. Once you work out how to communicate with your students, you will then be able to get the best out of them in each lesson. Connection is the tool that will enable you, as the teacher, to form a relationship with your students, where they will be able to identify with what and how you are teaching them. There is no clear right or wrong when it comes to teaching. There are, however, some things you can do that will work better than others. Ultimately, you need to aim to achieve connection with every single one of your students.

Learn to Identify Individual Personalities Within the Class

Each of your students will generally fall into one of 5 main personality categories, which you will learn to identify and differentiate. Once you understand the personality traits of your students, you can then implement strategies that will change the whole dynamic of your classroom.

These personality traits are:
1. The students who are excited: These are the students who almost can't contain their joy and enthusiasm.
2. The students who are content and comfortable: These are the students who feel safe, know what they need to do and do it with a smile.
3. The students who are constantly seeking attention: These students continually strive for your attention, want to be the centre of attention and have a tendency to speak over others, including you and other teachers.
4. The students who are shy and nervous: These students are a little uncertain, but trust you enough to listen to what you are saying; they are just not ready to contribute to conversations and ideas yet.
5. The students who are anxious: These students will often have extreme difficulty separating from their parent, joining in or contributing. This is more common in younger students; however, it still does occur with older students.

You will need to tweak your approach (sometimes ever so slightly) towards individual students, to best include, manage and teach them effectively.

Planning and Preparation

Next, there is a whole new element for you to master, aside from choreographing a dance or putting together a production. You now need to spend some time (before getting to class) planning and preparing for your lessons. Being prepared and planning in advance adds professionalism, as well as paves the way for students to make steady progression and improvement. (Remember, your students' progress also reflects on you as their teacher.)

I know some teachers will say, 'I don't need to plan, I can make it up on the spot'. But ask yourself this: Are you adequately meeting learning outcomes, observing progression and seeing results from your students if you do this?

When planning your lessons, you need to consider what the aim of your class is and the specific teaching program you are going to deliver in order to achieve that. Know the skill level, experience and age of your students. Use safe progressions that are logical and suitable for them. Most importantly, consider the emotional, physical and intellectual development of your students.

Communication

An essential skill for any teacher to develop is excellent communication. When you think about communication, know that it includes so much more than just talking. Once you become aware of the different variations of communication, you will notice a significant improvement in your connection to your students, and the impact you have on them and their growth. Ineffective communication opens the door for confusion and misunderstanding. This can lead to students feeling unsettled, disrupting others or being unable to stay focused during the class.

Essential communication skills that will significantly impact your teaching include:

1. Listening: Being a good listener is essential to being a good communicator. Practise active listening. Active listening involves paying close attention to what another person is

saying. One way to help you with this is to ask clarifying questions. So, after a student has said something to you, rephrase back to them what they said and ask them if you have heard and understood them correctly. Through active listening, you can better understand what the other person is trying to say and then you can respond appropriately.

2. Non-verbal communication: Non-verbal communication includes a combination of body language, eye contact, hand gestures and tone, which – together – help convey a clear understanding of your message. For example: a relaxed, open stance and a friendly tone will help you appear approachable and will encourage others to speak openly with you. Eye contact is extremely important. If it is culturally appropriate (in some cultures it may not be), look your student in the eye to demonstrate that you are focused on them and the conversation you are having with them. By using your eyes, smile and body gestures, it will encourage your students to engage in open and honest communication with you.

3. Be clear and concise: Set clear expectations, boundaries and rules in your classroom and explain to your students why they are there. For example: 'There is no running in the studio because you could trip over and hurt yourself or someone else'. If your students know why you have these expectations, boundaries and rules, they are more likely to respect them and you. When talking to your students, adapt your language and position yourself so you are at the same level as them. If they are sitting on the ground, then sit down with them. If they are standing, stand and talk to them. This way they will be able to engage and listen to what you are saying to them.

4. Empathy: Go into any conversation with a flexible, open mind and be ready to listen to and understand the other person's point of view. There are going to be times when you don't agree with what a student says, but it is important for you to

understand and respect their differing viewpoint. Using phrases such as: 'I understand where you are coming from, however ...' or 'I'm sorry you feel this way, however ...' demonstrates that you have been listening to what they have said and that you respect their opinions and views, but you don't agree.

5. Feedback: Learn how to master the art of delivering feedback and the importance of giving it to your students, as well as receiving it for yourself. Regular words of encouragement, tips for improvement and constructive criticism will enable your students to continue to develop and progress. It's also a great way to keep them motivated and wanting to try hard for you.

Listen to feedback given to you. It is such a gift to receive if someone (who is qualified) offers you some words of advice to help you improve. Ask clarifying questions if you are unsure of the issue and make an effort to implement the change.

Trust and Respect

Once you master these communication skills (which takes time and practise), it presents the opportunity to develop mutual trust and respect with your students. When you realise the power of mutual respect, your relationship with your students, their parents and your peers will change in the most positive way.

Respect your preschool-aged students as much as you respect your seniors. You will see a trust and bond form between yourself and your students, therefore making your role as their teacher a lot easier and more enjoyable.

Regardless of the age of your students, the style or genre you are teaching, and even your own teaching or dance experience; when it comes to trust and respect, it is a skill that will enhance your impact forever.

Know the power of your language and the words you use. You are shaping these humans.

This brings me to our final point in your teacher stage, which is about knowing how to keep your kids safe.

Keep Your Kids Safe

As teachers, we have an obligation to every single child and young person who walks into our classroom, to protect and keep them safe.

As you are no doubt aware, there have been some serious incidents in the media about sexual abuse of students by dance teachers. It is a sad and harsh reality; however, we have the power to make a difference and help keep our dancers safe.

You are obligated as the teacher to know the reporting procedures if you witness, observe or are told about an incident by a student. Check the studio's policies and procedures manual, as this should include the proper reporting process required.

There are different types of abuse that you need to be aware of. These include physical, emotional, verbal and sexual abuse, as well as bullying, discrimination and sexualisation. If you are unsure whether you should or shouldn't report an incident, then ask someone senior to you or contact your local government child safety agency.

When it comes to safe dance practice in and around the studio, be aware of the physical, environmental and emotional safety of your students. Know the difference between prevention and management for injury and risk. Ensure you implement and share your knowledge with your students to avoid short and long term injury and damage to their bodies.

The teacher stage is where you will experience soul-fulfilling growth and awareness. I know many amazing teachers who absolutely thrive in this stage.

Once you have accomplished these steps, you are ready to move into Stage 3, where you now become a mentor.

Stage 3 of the Evolution Model: Mentor

The Cambridge English Dictionary defines a 'mentor' as:

A person who gives a younger or less experienced person help and advice.

After your years of learning, teaching and training, you now have the opportunity to share your knowledge, time and experience – not only with your students, but with younger and newer teachers as well.

You will:

- Help the younger teachers and students develop useful attitudes, knowledge and skills
- Inspire them with vision, hope and possibilities for greatness
- Provide positive and constructive feedback, sharing your belief about what needs to be improved and offering suggestions
- Open doors to opportunities that may present in their future

Develop Leadership Skills

John C. Maxwell defines leadership this way: 'A leader is one who knows the way, goes the way, and shows the way.'

As leaders in the dance industry, the qualities you need to harness are to:

- Inspire others
- Be committed and passionate about your students and younger teachers
- Possess confidence, assertiveness and decision-making capabilities
- Be an exceptional communicator
- Include creativity and innovation
- Display honesty and integrity
- Be empathetic

Remember your 'why'! Why did you start to dance all those years ago? Why did you choose to teach dance? Why do you want to lead and become a mentor to others? These questions will help remind you of your passion and purpose, and guide you as a mentor.

Train and Guide Other Teachers

You now have an opportunity to train and guide other teachers. This responsibility needs to be taken seriously.

An important skill you need to master is how to give and receive feedback appropriately. By providing regular verbal feedback to younger teachers in a respectful way, you will help them develop into better teachers. Praise and encouragement, along with constructive feedback, will help them to excel. If delivered correctly, you will see them light up inside with pride and want to try harder. This is also a great way to keep everyone motivated.

Be sure to deliver constructive feedback honestly and deliver it with empathy and kindness. If there is an area of concern that needs addressing, organise a meeting to discuss the issue. Have an alternative solution in mind for the teacher to try when resolving the issue. As a mentor, you want them to succeed, so you need to help them by giving them some tools to use.

Actions speak louder than words. Set an example of respect to all other dance teachers and studio owners. Don't get involved in gossip or feed into negative rumours at any time. This includes with students, parents or other teachers.

Share Your Knowledge and Experiences

Embracing the opportunity to share your knowledge and experience among your team improves the quality of their teaching. Encourage newer teachers to take advantage of the more experienced teachers around them by observing their classes and the way they communicate with their students.

Gently remind your students and younger teachers to appreciate any mentor who takes the time to help them or offer advice. They are only providing feedback because they care and want to help them become a better dancer or teacher.

Some of the best lessons for you to share are your experiences and strategies that didn't work. Sharing times of challenge or failure – and how you managed them – can often be the best lesson for others because they can relate and laugh along with you, while learning from it at the same time.

Give Your Time to Other Less Experienced Teachers

No one understands the life of a dance teacher more than your peers. Make time to share your stories. Others will respect you more for doing so, plus they'll learn much quicker through your experiences. Another benefit is that you create an atmosphere conducive to a positive learning environment.

Be a positive role model. Share your love for your art with energy and enthusiasm. Use language that is respectful to other teachers, students, parents and peers, and always teach safe dance principles.

Your goal is for teachers and students to respect each other and respect the rules and policies of the studio, so you – as a mentor – need to set the standard.

Share More Than Your Dance Experience

You want your students and younger teachers to excel, so show and tell them how by sharing more than just your dance experiences. Share stories of your wins and losses, mistakes and learning. Allow them to know that this is a journey and it's not always going to be a smooth ride and, most importantly, that it is completely normal and okay.

The best way for any of us to thrive as a dance teacher is to be aware of our own strengths and weaknesses. Share these too. Ensure your students and younger teachers know the importance of being self-aware, so they can identify where they need to spend time gaining experience and developing their skills and training.

Other topics you can share and discuss are:
- The journey that lead you to your career
- Your 'why' and the reason you love doing what you do
- Their 'why': why they have chosen to pursue a career in dance
- How to stay motivated throughout the journey: Let them know there are going to be ups and downs, good times and

tricky times, but it's how they handle these situations that will determine their success

Nurture Your Students as Well as Younger Teachers

Whether this means building rapport through training days or social events, or merely offering a listening ear – this is now part of your obligation when taking on a mentoring role.

Your choice of words and your body language that accompanies them make a big difference in the message you send. Avoid harsh, judgmental words or a sarcastic tone. Ignoring someone can be just as detrimental to his or her self-esteem as a negative comment. So be aware of what you say and how you communicate it to your students and younger teachers, and deliver it positively.

You are responsible for the emotional and physical well-being of the students and teachers you mentor. This will often extend outside of the studio with issues that may occur at home or school. Take the time to listen and offer guidance and advice if appropriate. You may very well be their 'safe person', and the studio may be their 'safe place'.

Embrace a Wider Personal Approach

At this mentor stage, you now have more control over your time and where you choose to spend it.

Remember to expect the unexpected and be prepared to handle it graciously. Remain calm and flexible. Listen to your instincts, because they are usually right.

Don't let small issues or problems fester into bigger dramas. My advice is to put out any 'spot fires' as they occur. Don't be afraid to respectfully approach someone if you have any concerns or simply want to bring something to their attention. Something I say to my teachers, students and their parents is, 'Things can only be fixed if I know they're broken'. Encourage this type of open communication.

The way someone reacts or responds is usually a result of something going on in their life that you may not be aware of. So, handle all situations with a calm and flexible approach. Remain empathetic and understanding when dealing with tricky situations.

Becoming a mentor is something to be really proud of. However, it is not for everyone. It takes a specific type of person to embrace the responsibility of real leadership. If that's you – well done!

This brings us to the final stage where you transition into Stage 4 and become an industry leader.

Stage 4 of the Evolution Model: Industry Leader

Being an industry leader means you have acquired complete knowledge and skills within the student teacher, teacher and mentor stages. It is now time to think and dream big, knowing you have the potential to impact hundreds, if not thousands, of people.

Do Your Time

You can confidently move into Stage 4 once you have put in the hours over many years working in the industry, where you have been working on your own personal development, communication, people management and the art of connection.

Be confident within yourself that you can now share your knowledge and thoughts to add value to others in the industry.

Continue Your Own Higher-Level Training

It is a big responsibility to deliver advice, training and learning to many people who look up to you. It's just as important that you take the time to continue your own higher-level training. Many people at this level have their own mentor or coach – either business or personal. They are acutely aware of the benefits of obtaining support and guidance from those with even greater knowledge than themselves.

Earn Respect as an Authority Figure in the Industry

It takes time to earn respect as a person of authority in the industry. When you give to others, do kind things, offer your time and share your expertise without any expectation of getting anything back in return, people will see the impact you have and respect you for it. People posting, commenting and sharing their thanks, gratitude and personal experiences as a result of your actions is social proof that you have helped, inspired and influenced others in a positive way.

Know Who You Are and Who You Are Not

Being self-aware and practising mindfulness plays a big part in your success once you become an industry leader.

Mindfulness is being aware of everything around you, including the thoughts, actions, responses, and feelings you have for yourself and for people around you. Mindfulness improves focus, creativity and relationships as you consciously embrace and use empathy in making decisions and taking action. Essentially, you are more aware of yourself and you can read other people more accurately.

Personally, you can identify and come to a place of peace with who you are and who you are not. You will continue to consciously become a better version of yourself and the teacher you genuinely want to be.

You should have excellent communication skills and be able to converse assertively with confidence – not only towards your students, but also with other teachers, peers and people around you.

Adopt a Mindset of Giving, Helping and Making a Change for the Better

Finally, and probably most importantly, is for you to adopt a mindset of giving, helping and making a change for the better.

Understand and respond to the industry's needs, as well as the needs of individuals within the industry. Respond effectively to others with empathy and understanding.

You need to understand yourself, exercise self-care and compassion and, in doing so, be able to teach with kindness, care and positivity. Remain authentic, genuine, true to yourself and make positive choices.

Once you have done the hours over years of hard work, you become a true master. As talked about by Matthew Syed in his book,

Bounce – How Champions are Made: 'It takes 10,000 hours to achieve mastery. So now is a great time to start.'

Recap:

What you need to achieve at each stage of the 4-Stage Evolution Model:

The Student Teacher: Stage 1

- Complete your technical training
- Experience as many different genres and teaching styles as you can
- Develop a good work ethic and think beyond what's expected

The Teacher: Stage 2

- Put your training into practice
- Focus on developing connection with your students
- Embrace planning, preparation and classroom management

The Mentor: Stage 3

- Develop your leadership skills
- Share your knowledge and experiences
- Embrace a more comprehensive personal approach for your career

The Industry Leader: Stage 4

- Complete the hours (and years) of your own learning, teaching, mentoring and experience
- Deliver and receive a higher-level of training
- Earn respect as an authority figure in the industry
- Act as a leader in moving the industry forward

These are the 4 stages of the evolution process. I want to encourage and challenge you to really evaluate where you are right now and where you are heading so that you can start your journey doing what you love, sharing your passion with others and genuinely impacting young dancers everywhere.

Whatever stage you are at and wherever you see your career heading, know that you are well on your way to stepping into mastery if you are willing to do the work.

In the following chapters, I'm going to take you through the 5 Principles of Dance Teacher Mastery, which will guide you on your way to becoming an exceptional teacher and taking your career in whatever direction you desire it to go.

Chapter 2
Embracing Your Mastery

For me, embracing mastery requires you to be focused, disciplined and to have a burning desire to become exceptional at what you do. For you, in this case, it would be striving for mastery as a dance teacher.

Everyone's idea of mastery will be different. And it will be different depending on what season of your life and career you are in. It is an evolving process, but it is essential in order to enable your life and career to continue to grow and change.

The Oxford English Dictionary defines 'mastery' as:

1. Comprehensive knowledge or skill in a particular subject or activity.
2. Control or superiority over something.

To achieve mastery requires you to have self-discipline and motivation to focus on the processes and habits of learning every day so you can excel at something that means a lot to you.

So, let's break that down for you – the dance teacher …

The first thing we need to be clear about is that we are talking about you as a *teacher* – not a dancer.

Many amazing dancers have come to me for a job, but once they get in front of the students – boy, do they struggle to teach. This is because there is a difference – a big difference – between being an excellent dancer and an excellent teacher, which is okay – but you need to be aware of it.

Over my years of training teachers, I have identified 9 attributes that exceptional teachers are able to harness before they step into mastery. As a teacher, gaining these attributes will allow you to continue learning and growing to become an exceptional teacher, mentor and industry leader.

The 9 Attributes of Exceptional Teachers

1. Developing mastery: The first attribute that any exceptional teacher needs is to have worked hard over a period of time to develop mastery in their teaching. This forms the foundation of an exceptional teacher and everything else comes from this foundation.

2. Mistakes happen: Know and accept that you are going to make mistakes along the way. This is a good thing because it demonstrates you are trying new things and challenging yourself and your beliefs, which is how you grow. Learning from these mistakes helps you to do better the next time, which ultimately contributes to your overall growth and development.

3. Upskill to become unlimited: Your earning potential will be limited if you are just a dance teacher, so you need to take a more holistic approach to your career. You'll make money by sharing your knowledge, instilling your passion, and adding incredible value to the lives of your students.

4. Thinking with intention: Know that when you walk through the studio doors, you will be giving more to your students than just the steps you teach them. Think beyond what the students' *think* they need, to give them what you *know* they need. Is it confidence? Is it understanding? Or is it that they need to be challenged?

5. Perspective and empathy: See things through your students' eyes. Take a step back and think about how they may be assessing a situation. You will not necessarily see it the same way, but this gives you the ability to handle things with respect

and kindness, continually adding value to their lives. You can tell a lot about a person by how they treat other people, and it doesn't go unnoticed.

6. Value every student equally: Every student is going to bring something different to your class. Sometimes this will resonate with you and other times it will not. Your students play a significant role in your life and enable you to continue growing and developing your teaching skills. Value everyone you encounter along the way, because you wouldn't be where you are right now without them.

7. The art of caring: To quote author, Maya Angelou: 'Your students won't care how much you know until they know how much you care.' Take a genuine interest in your students, not only in your classroom, but beyond into their personal life as well. By truly caring and taking the relationship to a deeper lever, you will connect with your students, enabling them to open up and give more through dance.

8. Understand the responsibility of leadership: You don't need to have a title or position to practise leadership; however, you do have an obligation to serve. A great leader takes something that's complicated and makes it simple by explaining it in words and through actions. When you tell your students what to do, you focus on their weakness; when you show them how you work, and act as a positive role model, you focus on their strengths.

9. Know that your attitude is what holds the power: Two things you have control of in your life are your attitude and how you respond to different people and scenarios. Be encouraging and supportive, and do and be your best. Remember to keep adding value to your students in every interaction you have with them.

If you work on building these attributes into your life and career every day, you are then able to reach mastery, regardless of what stage of your career you are at.

Embracing Leadership

I was always destined to teach. Growing up, one of my favourite things to play was 'schools'. Every time we'd play (which was weekly), I'd rope my brother and cousin into being my students, while I – every single time – was the teacher. I wrote on the blackboard and gave out homework and assignments. Even back then, I planned out each lesson – spelling words, art class, music class and, of course, playground duty (where I walked around holding a mug filled with water, wearing pretend glasses and my mum's high heels, just like my teachers at school).

It was the same when we'd play 'dance class'. I was always the teacher. I decided on the songs, the choreography and the costuming. Once again, my 'students' did as I suggested.

When I think back, I realise I didn't even ask if anyone else wanted to be the teacher (oops)! But I also don't recall them asking. It was always just assumed that I was going to be the teacher.

Occasionally, I hear people referring to this type of behaviour as bossy or dominating. My concern here is that this projects a negative connotation for any young child displaying these types of leadership qualities. It frustrates me because, as I sit here many years down the track, it is clear that these behaviours were natural instincts for me. I am a leader and it's always been a part of me to want to take charge and make a difference in other people's lives.

So, my next question is: Why do only some people seem to possess these qualities to succeed at leadership, and others do not? I believe a significant contributing factor to one's success as a leader is determined by how their leadership qualities are harnessed as they are growing up by the people around them, and whether or not they are encouraged to view these traits as a positive thing.

Everybody is a leader in some way and, even at student teacher level, elements of leadership will stand out. Factors such as thinking ahead and pre-empting a situation, showing initiative, volunteering and supporting others are the beginnings of real leadership.

You don't need to have a title or position to practise leadership. I have trained a lot of assistant teachers over many years and I can tell you that age and experience aren't the determining factors for what makes a great leader.

I had a gorgeous teacher, Bella, who at the time was 14-years-old. She was respectful, grateful and helpful, and she continually demonstrated great initiative. I would watch Bella interact with the younger students and see how she would comfort them if they were feeling uncertain. I would observe her pick up rubbish from the studio floor and wipe up spilled water. No one asked her to do it, it was not expected that she did it, but she did it anyway. She didn't look around to see if anyone was watching and she wasn't waiting for praise or recognition at the end, she just did what needed to be done. I could see then that this young teacher had an incredible future ahead of her in whatever she put her mind to.

From time to time, I will deliberately monitor my assistants and my senior teachers from a distance, so they don't know I'm watching them. It still excites me when I see my staff going above and beyond, even when they are not aware they are being watched.

These are the makings of a true leader, and we need to nurture these qualities.

Embracing Influence

We see and hear so much about influencing and influencers on social media these days. Social media influencers are people who have a big following or big brand exposure, or they may even be minor celebrities who work for particular brands in the hope of convincing and persuading us to buy and use the products they are advertising.

Influence plays a significant role in your teaching. You make an impact and have an impression on your students, peers and the industry; so, whether you like it or not, you too are an influencer. Influence for you as a dance teacher is about being able to connect with and inspire your students. However, it also comes with an element of responsibility.

Leadership is about influence. So, how do you increase your influence? You raise your influence by intentionally adding value to each and every one of your students, through knowing their 'why' and how you can give them exactly what they want and need.

Your students each have gifts; you just have to find them. 'And how exactly do you do that?' I hear you ask. The answer is simple: by *connecting* with them. Once you've identified their gifts, you can then inspire, influence, transform and change their lives.

Recap:
Harness the 9 Attributes of Exceptional Teachers

1. Developing mastery
2. Mistakes happen
3. Upskill to become unlimited
4. Thinking with intention
5. Perspective and empathy
6. Value every student equally
7. The art of caring
8. Understand the responsibility of leadership
9. Know that your attitude is what holds the power

Embrace Your Leadership

A great leader takes something that's complicated and makes it simple. When you tell your students what to do, you focus on their weakness; when you show them *how* to do something, you work with their strengths.

Embrace Your Influence

You will make an impact and impression on your students and peers in the industry, so make sure it is exceptional.

Chapter 3
The 5 Principles of Dance Teacher Mastery

Very early on in my teaching career, I remember being given some compelling words of advice that I still hear in my mind every time I step in front of a class. These words came from my dad as he stood next to me at the side of the stage. This advice indeed influenced the type of teacher I am today, and is the same advice I continue to share every time I train new teachers.

It was stage rehearsal day for our end-of-year concert. There were excited dancers everywhere among a sea of sequins, playlists and running orders (handwritten on cardboard it was that long ago)! The day was running smoothly – well, as smoothly as stage rehearsal day can go, anyway. During each dance, I stood to the corner of the stage checking the spacing, positioning and the dancers' faces to make sure they were smiling.

It came time to run the finale. (It was to the song 'Shout' from Sister Act, to give you an idea of how long ago I'm talking about here!) At the end of the finale, the dancers were all so pumped and excited. The first words out of my mouth when they finished were, 'That wasn't too bad'. Then I began to wrap up the day. When I walked to the side of the stage, my dad asked me, 'So, was it not too bad or not too good?' At first, I didn't understand what he was asking, so he said it again, 'Was it not too bad or not too good?' It was then he said to me the words I will never forget, 'Those kids have danced their hearts out today and were so excited that you could not have wiped the smiles off their faces, but as soon as you said the words, "That wasn't too bad", their energy dropped'.

I had never thought about it that way before. I had never realised how my words so easily affected them emotionally. It was almost like they felt they had disappointed me or not lived up to my expectations of them. This couldn't have been further from the truth. It was simply the case that I didn't realise the power of my words and how everything I say controls the connection between my students and I.

From that point on, I never used words like that again. I became obsessed with finding words and actions that would give my students the feedback they needed to continue to improve each week – but delivered in such a way that they never felt worthless or incapable, just eager to keep learning and growing. And this knowledge, my friends, will raise you up to be an exceptional teacher.

Some of you want to teach as a career, some want to open a studio, while some of you will simply be happy to get a job and earn money doing something you love. Whatever it is for you, you need to be different and you need to stand out to step into mastery at the level you've chosen.

The 5 Principles of Dance Teacher Mastery

Principles are a foundational guidance system, which determine consequences and outcomes of situations, actions, responses and behaviour.

The 5 Principles of Dance Teacher Mastery are crucial in order for you to create a sense of purpose and progression in the lives of every student you teach, while staying focused on your values and goals to ensure you are the best teacher possible.

Principle 1: Awareness

Principle 2: Planning and preparation

Principle 3: Connection and communication
Principle 4: Creativity in the classroom
Principle 5: Professional and personal development

It doesn't matter where you are currently in the 4-Stage Evolution Model, as each of these 5 principles is applicable at every stage.

Principle 1: Awareness

Awareness of self and awareness of your students:

Self: Firstly, when it comes to yourself, the best way for you to thrive is to be aware of your own strengths and weaknesses, know what you love and what you don't, and get really clear on your personal and professional values, hopes, dreams and goals. By being self-aware, you can identify where you need to spend time developing your skills, training and gaining experience.

Students: The power in being aware of your students is that it allows you to start the crucial process of connection, meaning you begin to really understand your students, respond to their needs and relate effectively to them with empathy. It is then, and only then, you are able to bring out the best in your students. They will dance with conviction and passion, and give you their absolute best – all because of the connection you have developed by being aware of each of them as individuals.

Principle 2: Planning and Preparation

Benjamin Franklin so wisely said in his iconic statement: 'By failing to prepare, you are preparing to fail.' Planning your classes and having a structure in place (even if it's a loose structure) ensures you challenge, progress and extend your students in each lesson.

Preparation reduces the stress and overwhelm, not only for your students, but also for you. Planning and preparation demonstrates you respect your students' dedication and time and, in return, they will respect you and your commitment. It is another crucial ingredient in gaining a connection with your students.

Principle 3: Connection and Communication

Your choice of words and your body language make a big difference in the message you send to your students. Your goal as the teacher should be to establish positive self-esteem and share your passion for dance with the students, regardless of their skill level.

It doesn't matter the age, gender, experience or ability of your students, you need to recognise them as individuals; hence different teaching techniques and skills will work for some students and not for others. It's part of your role as the teacher to identify what each student needs and then implement strategies that will help you both!

When a teacher develops this skill, there is an enormous shift in the way classes run. Most importantly, the growth and progress of their students increases. You raise the morale in your classroom and then you are able to build your students up, which is really powerful ... but more on that later.

Principle 4: Creativity in the Classroom

I love challenging my teachers to continually raise their own 'barre' and think outside the 'stage' (square)!

I'm not only talking about choreography or costuming, I'm also talking about delving deeper into the whole experience for their students. Things such as getting their students to contribute to and be part of the creative process, challenging them to use indirect ways with positioning and corrections, thinking of ways to continually inspire their students to want to be better and give them (their teachers) everything they can.

Becoming complacent is dangerous (and a whole lot of hard work for you in the long run). You want to keep your students in the dance world as long as possible, so you have to continually think of new and exciting ways to achieve that.

Principle 5: Professional and Personal Development

It is so important that dance teachers and educators are always continuing to extend themselves, both professionally and personally. If you stop learning, you stop growing. In this industry, especially, it is crucial you keep up to date with not only the newest choreography and music, but also legislation and industry recommendations for the safety of your students and yourselves.

I'm not only talking about enrolling in courses or taking dance classes in the summer (though these are great things to do). Remember, you will learn something from everyone you come into contact with, whether it is a great idea for you to try or something you now know not to do! Whatever the lesson, these are the things that will keep you improving, growing and on the path to becoming a better teacher … and a better human!

Still, now, in my role as a studio owner, I am lucky to meet many wonderful young people who are passionate and keen to teach; however, it doesn't always have the fairy-tale ending you think it will. Young teachers not only have to want to teach, but they also have to want to *learn*.

Teaching is hard work and, if you do it correctly, it's more than just turning up and teaching students some choreography. In the beginning, the love for what you do needs to be worth more than your pay cheque.

You will need to put in a lot of hours of unpaid work if you genuinely want to be successful as a dance teacher. However, if you trust the process, listen to others who have been there and learn from their mistakes; you will get there, just as one of my teachers has …

Let me tell you about Tash.

Several years ago now, I was lucky enough to meet a talented, passionate and driven young dancer by the name of Tash.

She had a very clear vision for her future. The first time we met she told me she was going to own her own studio someday. Not only did she say this, but she also had a business plan, a business name picked, a picture of how her studio would look and details about how she wanted it to run to back up her words (and, by the way, she was only 14-years-old at this time)!

I was lucky enough to have Tash join our team as a student teacher, where I was able to mentor, teach and guide her for several years. Her enthusiasm was infectious and it impacted not only me, but also her peers and our students.

We would meet regularly to touch base. Tash would have a pad of paper with notes and ideas written down (which was incredibly pro-active for someone her age). I can't tell you how much I respected her for that!

The difference with Tash compared to many others I have worked with over the years is that she listened. She listened to what I said to do, she trusted that what I was telling her would work (and that I had learnt this from my mistakes in the past) and, most importantly, she *implemented* what I talked to her about.

A little side note here: I was always open-minded and loved hearing her ideas and suggestions, too. Some of these were great and worked well, but – on the whole – her success came down to her trusting the process and, more importantly, trusting me to guide her through it!

Tash is now into her third year of running her own studio and currently has 270 students, who she has organically attracted and retained by embracing the 9 Attributes of Exceptional Teachers (covered in Chapter 2) and implementing the 5 Principles of Dance Teacher Mastery we've covered in this chapter.

If you follow this program, you can be sure that you, too, are going to make an impact on your students and others within the industry, and that you will help shape them into who they are going to become.

So now it's *your* time to step into mastery.

In the next chapter, we'll dive a little deeper and explore the 5 principles in some more detail. We will discuss exactly what to do and how to do it, to take you from wherever you are now to your dream career that is awaiting you.

Recap:

To achieve mastery requires you to have self-discipline, motivation and focus on the processes and habits of learning – every day – so you can excel at something that means a lot to you.

Implement the 5 Principles of Dance Teacher Mastery

1. Awareness (of yourself and your students)
2. Planning and preparation
3. Connection and communication
4. Creativity in the classroom
5. Professional and personal development

Chapter 4
Principle 1: Awareness

*The better your awareness, the better your choices. As you
make better choices, you will see better results.*

Why do you teach or why do you want to teach? No, seriously ... I
want you to take a minute to *really* think about this question.

The reason it is important to identify your reason is because
teaching can be hard work. It's emotionally and physically draining.
The constant thinking, creating, assessing, re-assessing, the self-doubt,
and questioning every decision you make can be stressful at times. So,
why do you do it?

The answer is going to be different for each of us, but I can almost
guarantee that you are a highly sensitive, creative and passionate
person, and have a burning drive in you to share your soul with
others. Am I right? Can you imagine not being able to do the thing
you love so much?

Once you identify your 'why'– your reason for doing what you
do – everything becomes more natural and less like hard work. It
becomes easier to get out of bed, easier to sift through thousands of
songs to find the perfect one to suit that particular class, easier to put
in those hours of choreography and easier to turn up to work each
week to give so much of yourself to your students.

When it comes to teaching, there are no rules or guidelines to
dictate your creative process and delivery, but I'm going to give you

an idea of how to make your journey just that bit better, just that bit easier and just that bit more rewarding.

It all starts with Principle 1: Awareness.

I had a fantastic young teacher join our team several years ago. He was beautifully trained, still dancing himself and studying at a full-time school in the city. He was very keen to join our team and I was impressed with his initiative, so I organised a couple of classes for him to teach each week.

I gave him our senior students because I knew how much they would love the challenge of learning from someone young with fresh new ideas. The group of seniors had only recently moved into the level.

As this teacher started teaching the students, I noticed that he was throwing lots of tricky chore at them each week and moving through the routines really quickly. A couple of weeks into his teaching, two of our more confident and competent students approached me and told me they were feeling overwhelmed with how fast the class was moving and concerned that they were falling behind. I thought to myself that if these two students are feeling like this, surely others are too.

The problem was that he was teaching the students the chore *he* would want to be dancing, in the way *he* was currently being taught as a full-time student. He was not teaching at the appropriate level for the students' age, skill level and experience. Therefore, he was neglecting to assess himself and the way he approached his class.

Thankfully, after a chat, he was receptive to the feedback I gave him and started to teach for his students and not himself. He gained awareness into his situation (why it was not working for the students) and into himself (the way he worked with people).

Awareness is the perception, knowledge and understanding of a situation, circumstance or experience that is happening around you.

There are many benefits in being self-aware. It creates the pathway for you to consciously become the person and dance teacher you genuinely want to be. It will allow you to respond and act deliberately and appropriately, instead of reacting immediately and impulsively.

There are 3 areas of focus when it comes to awareness:
1. Yourself
2. Your students
3. The environment around you (within the studio and surrounds)

1. Awareness of Yourself

In the classroom, being self-aware will help you gain a greater understanding of your students' needs in order to respond with empathy and understanding. You will communicate with more confidence and assertiveness, as you make positive choices and remain authentic and genuine to yourself.

Your Values

Essentially, values are the things you believe are important in the way you live and work. When you identify your own values, you can use them to make more definite and precise decisions about your work and life.

Are you able to define your values? Do you know what they are? If you are unsure where to start, you can ask yourself the questions below and jot your answers down on a piece of paper.

When you are at your happiest in your life:
- What are you doing?
- Who are you with?
- What is it that makes you most fulfilled and satisfied?
- How and why does this experience or environment make you feel this way?

Once you've identified these things, make a list of the words that come to mind, which best represent them.
For example:
- Health – healthy food and exercise
- Family – immediate and extended
- Love – family and friends

- Creativity – at work
- Success – financial
- Honesty – in your communication
- Integrity – in your actions

Along with your personal values, it is important to also identify your professional values, as they play an essential role when it comes to the environment you chose to work in and the people you are surrounding yourself with. Aligning your professional values with the studio you work for will undoubtedly make for a more harmonious and enjoyable experience, because decisions will be based around shared beliefs and ideas.

Some examples of professional values could be:
- Exceeding expectations – for yourself, your students, your peers and your employer
- Thinking creatively to find better and more effective ways to teach
- Developing, investing in and improving yourself
- Taking initiative
- Taking responsibility and focusing on the outcome
- Kindness, compassion and positivity
- Respect and humility
- Happiness and fun – sharing your passion to bring joy to your students and yourself

Burnout

Many of you are working several jobs, studying and trying to balance the needs of a family at the same time as striving to excel in the classroom. Working long hours with a heavy workload will eventually catch up with you, which will make you susceptible to burning out. Fatigue, struggling to stay focused on tasks, continually getting sick, a lack of patience, insomnia and the loss of enjoyment in what you are doing, are all signs that you are on your way to burning out.

Prevention is undoubtedly better than a cure, so ensure you watch out for the warning signs and start getting into the habit of looking after yourself.

A self-care plan is a list of activities you love to do that aren't 'work', which make you feel good and have a positive impact on you. It may be going to the beach, reading a book, hanging out with friends or watching a movie. Include anything that makes you feel great. You need to schedule this self-care by having a plan. It is then easier to fit it into your week to ensure you take adequate time to rest and recuperate.

For me, I love getting a massage, going to the beach, taking a walk in nature, reading a good book or watching a movie. Find your 'things' so you can take some time to switch off your brain and relax.

Personal Development

Finally, when it comes to self-awareness and ensuring you continue to develop into the best teacher you can be, it's crucial you continue to keep learning and growing as a teacher and within yourself. Enrol or register for professional classes, courses or training that will extend your skills and knowledge. You can also share what you learn from these with your students and peers.

Keep up to date with changes in the industry, including legislation, industry recommendations, choreography and music.

Everyone you meet in life will teach you something, as will you when you engage with others. In your teaching capacity, it may be that you see a teacher using a different method of teaching in the classroom that you may want to try, or you may tweak a particular strategy you don't think is working very well to see if you can make it work better for you.

I also challenge you to take some time for self-reflection. Reflect on the way you are speaking to others and reflect on the way you are talking to yourself. How are you responding at times of stress or when you're feeling the pressure? With practise and experience, your ability to do this becomes more natural and comfortable, and it will enable you to re-evaluate everything that makes you a great teacher to turn you into an extraordinary teacher.

2. Awareness of Your Students

All interactions with your students will be slightly different, depending on many variables. Firstly, they are individuals so it's only human nature that they will respond differently than one other. But other factors will also have an impact, including how you're feeling on a particular day, what has happened before getting to class, how responsive your students are and what has happened during their day. These things will, in turn, affect the energy of the class. Even the weather can unsettle your students – throw the wind and a full moon in there and they can go crazy! Perhaps it has something to do with the ions being swirled around in the atmosphere, I'm not sure – but I do know my beautiful swans can very quickly turn into a pack of wild bears when it's windy!

Each student is different. You will understand that some students come into class easily, feeling content, comfortable and confident, while others will take time to adjust. If you are aware of this and know to expect it, then you will be much better equipped to deal with it when it happens.

Focus on creating a positive environment. If your students feel good, they'll give you more and try harder – they will want to impress you. Even for me, as I sit here with many, many years of experience training at the gym, I still love it when the instructor tells me I'm doing a good job. Let's be honest, I *know* I am doing well (as I should be after dancing my whole life), but it's still nice to *hear* it from someone else every now and then! The secret is to find your students' passion (even if it's not dancing) and connect with them through that.

A couple of years ago, I had a young boy join our all boys hip hop group. The teacher was struggling to get him to stay focused and listen during the lesson. I went to him and asked, 'Hey Lucas, what's your favourite movie?' He said, 'I love Karate Kid'. I responded, 'I love that movie too. It has some great songs in it. How about we do a combo to one of the songs from the movie next week?' His eyes lit up with excitement and he exclaimed, 'Yes! I can show you some of the moves I already do because I do them at home.'

Ever since that day, Lucas has been attentive and enthusiastic. So, by taking the time to listen to him and identify something he loved and could relate to, I was able to connect it to hip hop. He was happy and so was his teacher!

The lesson here is that when you pay attention and take the time to ask the questions, you can start to relate and connect to your students to find out the things that excite them. Even though, for most of us, it's dance that fills our soul; for some students, dancing is just one of their many interests, so you may need to find another road in to connect with them.

Be confident in yourself and your knowledge. Let me say that again. Be confident in yourself and your knowledge! Know that your relationship is going to be different with each of your students, but you will use the same core fundamentals for every single student you have the privilege of teaching.

Connection

Ultimately you are striving for connection with your students. It is then, and only then, you are able to get the best out of them. Connection is a core aspect of becoming an exceptional teacher.

Here are some things you can do to help encourage this connection:

- Make it a priority to know your students' names and, if possible, the names of their parents too. This will help you gain the respect of your students and their parents, help you control your class and make your students feel important. If a new student starts in your class, write their name down, so you remember it for the following lesson and will be able to greet them by their name. Your connection will be strengthened if your students are recognised and acknowledged by name.

- Include all students during the lesson and use eye contact when speaking to them. There will always be students who are shyer than others, and other students who will talk non-stop. Identify who these children are and give each student equal attention.
- Your choice of words makes a big difference in the message you send to your students. Avoid harsh, judgmental words or a sarcastic tone. Ignoring students can be just as detrimental to their self-esteem as a negative comment. Never dismiss an idea. Always listen and respond.
- Remember small things. If your students tell you about a holiday they are going on, something exciting that is happening at school or an achievement other than dance, ask them about it the next time you see them. They will delight in the fact you remembered.
- Take the time to notice and acknowledge the small details, for example: a neat ballet bun, a new dance outfit or new bag, or the fact they are trying really hard and smiling a lot this lesson. Noticing these things has a significant impact on your students, and their confidence will soar. The better they feel, the harder they will try for you and the more both you and your students stand to gain.

Knowing Their 'Why'

You now know your 'why', but have you stopped to think about your students' 'why'? Why do they turn up each lesson to learn how to dance? Is it that they are training to dance professionally or are they just looking to enjoy recreational classes? Have their parents sent them to dance classes to help build their self-confidence? Try to find this out about your students. Whatever their reason, you need to teach accordingly. Your approach to recreational students will be somewhat different than it is with your elite students. Although the teaching fundamentals are the same, there will be variations in expectations and outcomes.

Whatever you identify these to be, ensure their self-confidence is not jeopardised and their experiences are ones that allow them to grow.

The Role of Respect

There are a wide variety of studios across the world that will appeal to the wants and needs of an individual. Some of the different types of studios include elite, high-level performance and examination focused studios, or those that offer general, recreation classes aimed at dancers who are primarily seeking a fun lesson of dance once a week. Regardless of which type of studio you are teaching at, your focus should be to teach your students correct and safe technique, while building on their skill level and progressing them accordingly.

Include and respect each of your students. You will teach students who are at varying levels of their dance journey. When you realise the power of mutual respect, your relationship with them, their parents and your peers will change in the most positive way forever.

Respect your preschool-aged students as much as you respect your seniors and adults. If you do this, you will see a trust and bond form between you and them, making your role rewarding, fulfilling and enjoyable. Regardless of the age of your students, the style and genre you are teaching or your own teaching and dance experience – developing mutual respect will define your impact forever.

Don't make assumptions. Everyone has a story and could have something going on in their life that you may or may not be aware of. It could be financial concerns, family issues or maybe they have had a big fight with their best friend. You will never know the truth unless the information has been directly delivered to you. Teaching in a way that makes a student feel humiliated, guilty or ashamed will not benefit anyone and the student may not continue to dance because of this. You could just be their 'go to' person and the studio may be the place where they feel safe and happy, so don't compromise that trusted and privileged position.

If you, as a teacher, have concerns about a student missing class, turning up late or not wearing uniform, speak to the studio owner or their parent directly. Don't punish the student or ostracise them as they walk into your class. When you think about it, a student turning up late is usually not something they can control. Just be careful not to accuse or make them feel ashamed, because you don't know what else is happening in their life.

It's About Your Students – Not You

You should strive to ensure the classroom maintains a positive atmosphere, which promotes high morale in your students. This will affect the overall success of your goals and outcomes. Students who know you care about them will be much more likely to want to be the best dancers they can be – for you and for themselves. On the flip side, continually sending negative messages or comments to your students is detrimental to their education, self-confidence and belief, as well as your success as their dance teacher. Students who are made to feel that they are slow learners, not keeping up with the rest of the class or are more of a hassle than a pleasure to teach, will ultimately stop coming to avoid the negative feelings they experience in class.

It can be tricky and I think the reason it's so hard is that many teachers tend to value themselves based on the 'final product' or the 'results' of their teaching. For example: we strive to teach the correct technique, so it's performed by our students in polished routines for the public. This might be okay for students who have been training for many years with hours of practise behind them, but if you try and teach the same thing to newer students, the routine will look untidy. This could lead to the students losing confidence and, ultimately, you end up feeling deflated because they aren't pulling off the routine as you had visualised in your mind.

At the beginning of most teaching careers, I see teachers teaching what they would want to do if they were dancing the routine, instead of thinking about what will work best for the students they are teaching and meeting them at the level they are at.

Your goal as a teacher should be to establish positive self-esteem and passion for the art of dance in your students. Remember that every student can develop passion, regardless of skill level. Do everything you can to communicate that you believe each of your students will succeed.

For starters, smile! It's contagious and it offers your students comfort when you convey a sense of warmth, approval and care. It is one of many ways in which you can send the message that each student is competent and valued. You could also give compliments often, even if they're not about dance. Every child in every class has something to offer. For example: you might comment on a beautiful smile or commend a terrific effort. Treat your students the way you would have wanted to be treated by a teacher when you were their age and in the same position.

Identify what type of praise an individual student responds best to. Some children need a cuddle when they walk into the room, some need to be encouraged to speak and there will be some who need to be reminded about the rules and expectations in your classroom. It's your responsibility to make each of them feel welcomed, wanted and comfortable, and meet whatever their needs may be (with an understanding that they each have different needs).

Simply put, teaching is about your students and not you, so you have to set aside your ego and do what's best for them.

Personal Relationships and Social Media Behaviour

To avoid a conflict of interest or the perception of favouritism, it is best not to engage in a personal relationship with students or their parents. Young teachers who socialise with students in this way can lose the respect they need to be effective teachers and role models. The boundary of student/teacher relationships can quickly become blurred, making your job really difficult. Don't give your personal telephone number to students or their parents. All communication with teachers and staff should be made through the studio office if possible.

Are you aware of the boundaries and rules regarding social media, photographs, videos and sharing information? This will vary slightly depending on which studio you are teaching at, but be sure to ask the studio owner for the guidelines if you haven't already been informed.

Generally, you will find most studios are on the same page when it comes to this information. A lot of it is common sense, but I will still go through it with you below:

- You should not make any personal phone calls, send text messages, take photos, or use Facebook, Instagram or other social media platforms while you are teaching (except for emergencies or unless otherwise instructed to do so by the studio owner).
- Mobile phones (including your own) should be turned onto silent so they don't interfere with the learning. Generally, a studio policy would prohibit students from using mobile phones, tablets or computers during class time. Since you, as teachers, need to set an example, the same rule should apply to you (unless there is an emergency or you suspect a parent of one of the children is urgently trying to contact you).
- Generally, the studio owner should be the one to make all communication with students and parents. Most studio owners would discourage teachers from having contact with students or their parents without consulting with them first. This includes phone calls, emails, text messages, personal social-networking sites or socialising outside of class time. Once you start getting involved on a personal level with your students or their parents, it can lead to problems. If something was to go wrong between you and them, or you were accused of something inappropriate, it could become a really stressful and emotional rollercoaster. This is why it is best to have a clear rule of no personal contact.
- Under no circumstances should you take a photo or video of your students and upload it to any form of social media – again,

particularly on your personal social media accounts. There are strict rules preventing you from posting photos of anyone without their permission (particularly children). Our students need to be protected and safe, and their parents should feel confident that this is your highest priority when their child is in your care.

Camaraderie With Other Dance Studios

Respect all other dance teachers, studios and studio owners. Don't discuss rumours or get involved in gossip at any time with your students or their parents regarding any other school or teacher.

Remember one person's version of an event is always going to be weighted in their favour. There are three sides to every story: yours, the other person's and the truth. If you do hear rumours or gossip, stop it in its tracks right then and there. Shut the conversation down and don't let it build momentum. If you have genuine concerns, go straight to the source and ask. Teachers who speak negatively about others, whether inside or outside the studio, are not setting the right example to their students and their parents, or their peers. Simply remember your 'why' in all of your dealings.

3. Awareness of the Environment

Safety

You have a responsibility to keep your dancers safe. This includes the dancer themselves, as well as ensuring that the environment they are in is safe for them.

In an effort to keep your students safe:

- Communicate openly with your students, with an emphasis on creating a non-secretive environment.
- Ensure that every child is treated equally, with dignity and respect.
- Where possible, avoid working in a closed room or studio in a one-on-one situation with a child. This can be challenging if

you are teaching a private lesson and there are no other adults around. In the past, I have taught in community centres that don't have a viewing window or cameras. In situations like this, you need to use common sense to act in a safe and appropriate manner and minimise the risk of any misunderstandings from occurring. Look at creative ways to rectify the situation. Is it possible to leave the door slightly ajar? Is there someone who could sit in the back of the classroom during the lesson? The first thing to do is make sure the student, their parents and the studio owner are aware that you have identified the issue. Then ask for suggestions on the best way to handle it.

- Learn the indicators of abuse and how to respond if you become aware of, or suspect, that abuse is taking place. Signs could include a lack of trust in adults, poor self-image or self-esteem, acting in a secretive manner, demanding or disruptive behaviour, bruises or pressure marks in unlikely places (e.g. face, back, ears or hands), wariness of physical contact with others or promiscuous affection-seeking behaviour. For more information on this, you can check out this website: https://education.nsw.gov.au/student-wellbeing/child-protection/child-protection-policy-guidelines/resources

- Know what your obligations are should any concerns arise about the safety, welfare or well-being of any child. If you suspect something may be going on with one of your students or you are suspicious of another teacher or adult, speak to the studio owner to follow on with the complaint. Again, if you are unsure, you can check out this website for more information:

- https://education.nsw.gov.au/student-wellbeing/child-protection/mandatory-reporting

Safety in the Studio

Every time you walk into the studio, you need to be aware of the environment around you. When your students are in your care, you are responsible for their safety and well-being, so being aware of dangers or hazards around the studio is crucial.

In many circumstances, the dance space environment will be out of your control, so you need to make decisions for the dancers that will minimise risks (e.g. eliminate jumps on a hard floor, remove any objects that are in the way or could cause injury, ensure dancers wear appropriate dance clothes and footwear, and stay hydrated to compensate for the room temperature).

Each time you walk into the studio, scan the room on 3 different levels:

1. First, look across the floor level: Identify any trip hazards, spills, bags or furniture that may cause a student to injure themselves.
2. Next, scan the room at your eye level: Ensure that there isn't a picture that has come loose off the wall or that the barre doesn't have a nail protruding from it.
3. Finally, look up: Check all lights and fans are secured and that nothing could drop and cause injury to you or your students.

Food in the Studio

Food allergies and intolerances, which can be fatal, are becoming a lot more prevalent in our society. Be aware and stay vigilant in case a student brings food into the classroom that may cause an allergic reaction in another student. Know where the first aid kit is located in the studio (or better still, have your own that you carry in your dance bag) and be sure your first aid certificate is up-to-date in case an emergency or injury occurs.

Many of you will teach several classes in a row. You will need to snack and refuel your body during a long stint of teaching. This should be done discretely during a class changeover, not in the middle of your class or in front of your students. Also try to ensure you make healthy selections, as you will have eyes on you the whole time and you should aim to set a good example.

Another food that should not be allowed in the classroom is chewing gum (for both students and teachers). Apart from the dangers of choking, it looks unprofessional to be chewing gum when teaching.

In wrapping up this chapter, it is important to remember why awareness is the first of the 5 principles. It is because awareness forms the fundamental basis of which connection is formed. This includes the connection you have with the art of dance and why you have chosen a career in teaching others. It also includes the connection you have with your students and ensuring they are receiving exactly what they need, which ultimately impacts your career in teaching.

Recap:
Principle 1: Awareness

1. Awareness of yourself
   - Know your 'why'
   - Identify your values
   - Watch for the signs of burnout
   - Continue your own personal development

2. Awareness of your students
   - Work towards connection
   - Know their 'why'
   - The role of respect
   - Be aware of your social media behaviour and personal relationships

3. The environment
   - Safety
   - Safety in the studio
   - Food in the studio

Chapter 5
Principle 2: Planning and Preparation

Planning is the platform for growth and success.

I wish there was a sexier word for planning! Even though the word 'planning' doesn't sound earth-shatteringly exciting, the impact of actively planning across all areas of your life is!

I remember when I first started out teaching I never thought to plan out my lessons. I would have warm-up music and a song picked out for the concert dance, but that was it. I had no warm-up exercises, no technique or travelling steps, no chorography, and certainly no time management plans.

My downfall here was that I wasn't able to strategically progress my students each week due to a lack of preparation. I couldn't remember exactly what we did the lesson before and I didn't pace out teaching the choreography so, when it came time for their performance, my students weren't confident with the end of their dances because I didn't allow enough time to practise that section into their muscle memory. Apart from the students not feeling confident with their dances, I was also embarrassed that they didn't look as sharp and polished as I had wanted.

However, I did learn from these mistakes ... and I always ensure to highlight the lessons I've learned along the way to all the teachers I now train.

Some of you will find implementing planning and preparation into your work and life schedule easy, and some of you will not, but I do encourage you to try it out, regardless. Not only will it reduce stress and anxiety, but it will also help you meet the responsibility you have to your students to ensure they continue to progress and improve, by setting benchmarks and goals. To do this, there needs to be a clear and structured plan in place to ensure you reach them.

The things that will get you to where you want to go are:

1. Daily routines
2. Planning your daily to-do list
3. Effective time management
4. Organisation and systems

1. Daily Routines

Most successful and productive people start each day with a positive morning routine. Your daily routine is simply a structured list of things you do every single day so that your day is full of purpose and executed with intention. It will set the pace of your day and increase your productivity.

Things to include in your morning routine could be:

- Exercise/stretch
- Shower
- Meditate
- Journal
- To-do list

2. Planning Your Daily To-Do List

When planning out the things you need to do each day, start by making a list of what you need to do during the day. Then, put them in order of priority from most important to least important. It doesn't matter how many things are on your list.

Include the things you need to do for work (e.g. finding music, choreography and lesson planning), as well as the things you need to get done personally (e.g. doing your washing, getting a haircut and buying groceries).

3. Effective Time Management

Have you noticed that most times when you speak to someone and ask, 'How are you going?' they reply with, 'I'm so busy' (usually with an emphasis on 'so')? I have a little chuckle to myself every time I hear someone say it. Everyone's perception of busy is (of course) different and, as we've all heard numerous times before, everyone has the same number of hours in the day. However, I do wonder how others are managing their time and choosing to spend those 24 hours.

Some people sell the idea of time management as complicated, but it really isn't.

Just try starting like this:

1. Work out how much time (or blocks of time) you have in the day where you can work through your to-do list (e.g. it may be 10 am to 12 pm and 12.30 pm to 2.30 pm).
2. Make a list of the things you need to get done (refer to the list you previously made).
3. Prioritise and number them from most important/urgent to the least important/non-urgent and start working through from the top.

I like to put a deliberate line through each task as I finish them. It gives me a great feeling of satisfaction and accomplishment. And, I'm going to let you in on a quirky tendency of mine, just between you and I – I've even been known to add things to the list that I've already done, just so I can get the satisfaction of crossing them off!

When the next day rolls around, repeat the 3 steps again.

In most cases, we tend to put off the most laborious or least enjoyable task until last. But, procrastinating won't do you any favours so if you just knuckle down and get that one done, the rest of your tasks won't seem so bad and then you will have time for the fun stuff.

4. Organisation and Systems

Being organised and having simple 'life systems' will not only allow you to be more productive, but also help you look professional, prepared and calm, which is everything you should want to be as a dance teacher. Again, this will cross over from your personal life into your professional life, which is what we are going to talk about now.

Simple organisational tasks can include things such as packing your bag the night before, deciding what you are going to wear the next day and knowing what food you are going to eat.

Below is a list of ideas for you to try.

Pack your dance bag the night before with:

- Shoes
- Spare clothes
- Deodorant and make-up
- Music, including cords and adaptors
- Phone/tablet/laptop and chargers
- Back-up music source or batteries
- Syllabi/programs
- Props
- First aid kit
- Contact details in case of an emergency (e.g. studio owner, key holder and back-up teacher)

Nutrition:

- Water
- Snacks
- Have meals and snack options planned for long teaching stints

Clothes:

- Plan what you are going to wear
- Know how you are going to do your hair and make-up

Diarise time for self-care (more on that soon).

Being organised and able to manage your time well are great skills to master, which will spill over into your teaching. I challenge you to give it a go if you don't already do so.

Class Planning

Trust me when I say that planning is the platform for success and growth. Class planning refers to the strategies you put in place before entering the classroom so that you and your students don't become stressed or overwhelmed. Consider the approach you are going to take and how you plan to focus each particular group of students.

Some points you need to consider are:

- The aim of your class and the specific teaching program you will be using
- The skill level, experience and age of your students
- Using safe progressions that are logical and suitable for the class you are teaching
- The emotional, physical and intellectual development of your students

Lesson Planning

I know that sometimes, as creatives, the thought of planning out your lesson is unfathomable. Honestly though, when done right, it can change everything for the better.

Planning your classes and having a structure in place ensures you continue to move forward. Your students grow, learn and improve consistently, which is not only great for their self-esteem, but also a great connection and retention strategy for you.

Your lesson plan needs to include:

1. Aim/goal: What you would like your students to achieve by the end of the lesson?
   - A particular skill or step

- Improved confidence
- Strong technique and posture
- Strong rhythm and timing
- 32 counts of choreography for their dance

2. Warm-up:
   - Will it be teacher-lead or student-lead?
   - Starting position – lines or in a circle?
   - Include floor work
   - Drama/singing

3. Progressions and techniques:
   - Travelling combination
   - Group work
   - Improvisation
   - Syllabus work

4. Choreography:
   - New combination
   - Add 32 bars to the new routine
   - Practise existing routines
   - Student choreography

5. Cool-down:
   - Feedback to your students
   - Ask your students to reflect on what they've learnt
   - Stretch and breathing
   - Hydration

Lesson Structure

When you have mapped out your lesson plan, you can move onto the basic structure of the lesson.

Let's start with the timing breakdown of your lesson.

1. A 30-minute class will generally need to be broken into 3 lots of 10 minutes:
   - 10 minutes for warm-up/stretch
   - 5 to 10 minutes for wall/corner/new steps
   - 10 to 15 minutes for routine practise, new choreography and cool-down

2. A 45-minute class will generally need to be broken into 3 lots with:
   - 10 to 15 minutes for warm-up/stretch
   - 10 to 15 minutes for technique/combination
   - 15 to 20 minutes routine practise and new choreography

3. A 60-minute class will generally need to be broken into 3 lots with:
   - 15 to 20 minutes for warm-up/stretch
   - 15 to 20 minutes for technique/combination
   - 15 to 20 minutes for routine practise and new choreography

A good tip is to wear a watch or have your phone nearby so you are aware of the time. This is important so you can pace the class. If you do a quick warm-up and move straight into the dance, the students could get bored, either from repeating the routine over and over again or you giving them too much chore and them not being able to retain it. If you drag out starting the class, you'll end up panicking at the end of the lesson because you will run out of time to finish teaching them what you had planned. Your younger students will struggle to stay focused for more than 20 to 25 minutes doing the same thing so sticking to the basic time breakdown will help them to stay engaged.

If you feel as though your students are losing focus, try adding some variety to the lesson.

This could include:

1. If you have taught a new step or combination, ask the students to break into small groups and practise together while you walk around and assist. Continue with the music playing quietly in the background, so there is some noise.

2. Ask your students to break into groups and challenge them in their group to make up a quick combination for them to perform in front of the class.

3. Ask your students to improvise to a piece of music. This creates an atmosphere of creative energy and it encourages students to be confident in their own ideas.

4. Add drama, progressions and new steps into the lesson. Change the positions and directions of where your students are standing. This disrupts their thought patterns and assists in keeping their focus (e.g. ask them to stand along the wall, sit on the ground, stand in a circle, work with a partner or start from the corner). You'll have heard that a change is as good as a holiday ... okay, it may not be quite as good as a holiday but, without a doubt, the thought of something different and new can be exciting!

5. Depending on the age of the students, how many of them are in a class and how many teachers are in the class; ask students to demonstrate the steps on their own or in pairs. Always watch, correct and help them, and compliment their effort.

When it comes to your younger students, if you're teaching a new step, it can be a good idea to ask them to sit down to watch you demonstrate first. Once you have finished your demonstration and given them a clear explanation of what to do, ask them to stand and practise altogether.

Ending the Lesson

The way you end your lesson is just as important, if not more so, as the way you begin each lesson. Your lessons should end on a positive note. If your students leave feeling frustrated or deflated, they might think that dancing isn't their thing and decide not to continue.

Spend a couple of minutes giving students some feedback – constructive and positive – as well as asking them to reflect on what they just achieved, their personal accomplishments and what they are going to work on before you next meet again. This type of reflection could be verbal or written in a journal. There is great power when a dancer writes down their goals!

If you are hearing feedback about yourself or the way you are conducting a class, take it on board and do some self-reflecting of your own. Maybe there is a better way that you could be doing things? Don't get defensive. Remember, exceptional teachers never stop learning from their students either.

So there you have it! There is a lot of information for you to take in and consider. This lesson planning PDF will help you get on top of it. You can download it here: http://www.danceteachercentral.com/wp-content/uploads/2018/10/02-Lesson-Planning-and-Choreography.pdf.

Choreography

Every now and then, I still get surprised when a teacher isn't aware of something I assume all dance teachers would know. Since I am writing this book to help all teachers in varying stages in their career, I figured I would start at the beginning. Some of you may know this information already and have a system or process that works for you, but you may still be able to pick up some new ideas or different things to try, which could improve the way your lessons run.

1. Music
   Songs are generally 4/4 timing and contain verses and choruses. Your choreography needs to fit into the bars of the music (usually we count to 4 or 8 as dancers). The first beat of the bar is the strong beat, which is when we want to have a strong movement to emphasise the beginning of the bar.

For younger students, it's crucial that choreography is kept relatively simple and that the steps you teach are on the even count or strong beat of the music. If the choreography and timing are too intricate or complicated, it just becomes messy, as they are not yet experienced in hearing the beats and rhythms while moving at the same time.

2. Demonstration

A great skill to master, especially with younger students, is to demonstrate and teach facing them, so essentially it's like they are looking in a mirror. You face them, and while they are using their right arm or leg, you are using your left. This is indeed a skill that comes with practise – but I find it a great way to keep your students engaged and develop that connection I talk so much about, because you can look directly into their eyes as you teach them.

As students become more experienced, your choreography will become a lot more involved with timing, rhythm, cannons and positioning, but an exceptional teacher needs to master working with all levels of students – from beginner to elite.

3. Creating your choreography

Creating your choreography is personal and individual. We all like different things, which is a good thing because the industry would be pretty dull if it was all the same. Ensure you keep your creative juices flowing and your inspiration high. Take classes for yourself, be inspired by other choreographers, then add your own twist and flavour so that people fall in love with you and your style.

Please keep it age appropriate. Even for your older students – be classy, technical and skilled, not tacky and cheap!

When it comes to weekly classes, I truly believe that you need to be prepared. I have only seen a handful of teachers over the years that can flawlessly choreograph on the spot without hesitating or becoming distracted.

There is nothing worse than looking in the studio and seeing a teacher facing the mirror or the wall, listening to the song and trying to mark out choreography. It is so unprofessional. Aside from this, once you lose the focus of your students, it is very tough to get them back in the flow of things again. At a minimum, spend 10 or 20 minutes listening to your song of choice and know what you are going to teach before you get into the classroom.

4. A simple flow for teaching a routine or combination

Ask your students to spread evenly around the room. Like I spoke about earlier, for any of your younger students, try to face them as you are teaching, but ensure you are using the arms/legs that mirror theirs.

Run the dance or combination a couple of times with the music. Hopefully they remember it and you can move straight on, but that is certainly not always the case.

If they have forgotten, run through the choreography from the last lesson without the music. Once their memory has been refreshed, run just that section of the chore with the music.

Finally, run the whole dance from the beginning with music and then move onto the new chore for the week.

Another little tip is that if the students appear to be getting restless, offer a drink break so that they have time to absorb choreography and refocus.

I'm still 'old school' and like to write out my chore, but it doesn't matter whether you write it out, film it or remember it in your head, as long as you are prepared.

I know, too, that ultimately it is up to the students to remember what you taught them during the previous lesson, but sometimes they won't. I know how frustrating it can be and, if it is an ongoing problem, then there are other strategies you can implement to help rectify the situation. However, generally speaking, you should be able to refresh your memory before the lesson, refresh theirs quickly once you begin and then move on.

This, my friends, is another great reason to record it somewhere – so it's one less thing you need to remember!

Event Planning

In your teaching career there will be a variety of opportunities for your students to perform at events. Applying to have your students perform in all kinds of industry events opens them up to new experiences, challenges and opportunities. Some of the more popular ones are:

- Concerts
- Eisteddfods
- Outdoor performances
- Community events
- Charity events
- Dance expos
- Television and commercial filming

When it comes to events, I don't just have a Plan B; I also have a Plan C, D, E, F and G, because I've been caught out before!

During one of our concerts, there was a blackout halfway through. We had sold over a thousand tickets, it was a 35-degree day and we had hundreds of students backstage with no air-conditioning, lights or music! As a result of that incident, I'm now the proud owner of a portable generator that comes to every concert with me, just in case we have another power outage!

I also had an event where the teacher who was bringing the music for the performance had a car accident while on her way (thankfully she was okay), but I didn't have a copy of the songs with me. So now I always carry a USB, CD and a copy on my phone with it uploaded to Google Drive, so I will never be in that situation again.

Initially, the set-up may seem daunting and a lot like hard work, but once it's done, every event after that merely requires a simple tweak here or there.

As the teacher in charge, you need to plan in advance to ensure smooth running and professionalism every time.

A simple checklist you can use is to consider the following:

- Variables such as the weather, sound quality and where the parents need to wait
- Conditions, size and surface of the stage or performing area
- Parking or transport options
- Music source and availability of technology to play music
- Back-up music sources
- Dressing rooms
- Timing of actual event and rehearsals
- Additional costs to performers and parents on arrival
- What to pack (music, hand towel, bobby pins, hairspray, make-up, spare headpieces, brush and extra stockings)

Another suggestion is to have pre-formatted emails with event details that you can send out to the students, their parents and other teachers who may be involved with the event. Every event you attend will require similar information to be shared, so keep a general template and update it with specific details for each event. This will save you time and brain power, plus reduce the risk of missing any crucial information.

Looking After Yourself

After unpacking all the information in this chapter, I wanted to finish on this very important topic.

With all the planning and preparation in class, it is vital you remember and take care of *you* during the process.

Managing your energy, sleep and health needs to take priority or you will burn out. For now, start to identify the things that make you feel good, the things you love to do and the people who make you a better person.

For me, I love walking along the beach or in nature. I don't keep a big circle of friends, but the ones I have make me laugh out loud, bring out the best in me and are a joy to be around. I love spending time with my family and eating out at nice restaurants. Once you identify what those things are for you, ensure you regularly slot them into your usual, hectic life. Literally book them into your calendar, so you have to commit to doing them. You want to strive for a beautiful balance here.

The planning process may seem overwhelming at the moment, but it's not as complicated as it looks. Remember, the power of planning will change your life.

Planning and preparation are key elements in the development of mastery at whatever stage of professional evolution you are at, so if you don't already – start by implementing a daily routine, prioritising your to-do list and planning out your lessons to get the most out of your day, your career and your students.

Recap:
Principle 2: Planning and Preparation

- Make a habit of day-to-day routines that make managing your life easier and less stressful
- Plan your classes and have a structure to ensure your students grow, learn and improve consistently
- Be smart and creative with your choreography and how you teach your students, while keeping them engaged
- Create an Event Checklist that you can refer to for every event you attend, with only slight tweaking required each time
- Diarise time for yourself so you will keep operating at an elite level

Chapter 6

Principle 3: Connection and Communication

Communication and human connection are the keys to success.

Verbal communication and your body language (or non-verbal communication) are the ways you convey and express information and feelings. It is when you establish exceptional communication and body language skills that you develop an even more profound connection with your students.

Think about the wave you give to another driver when they let you merge in front of them, or the expression of pride you see from a teacher as they watch their students perform on stage for the first time. The feeling that you feel inside is the same as the feeling you are able to give your students with the way you express yourself. Once you become aware of exceptional communication, your body language and how others respond, these invaluable skills will aid you in becoming an excellent and exceptional teacher.

Classroom Connection and Communication

When it comes to classroom connection, you need to incorporate 5 elements of communication and body language in order to engage with your students and effectively convey your message.

These are:

1. Facial expressions and eye contact
2. Listening to understand

3. Empathy and feeling
4. Gestures and response
5. Voice, speech and the words you choose

1. Facial Expressions and Eye Contact

Smile – not only with your mouth, but also with your eyes. Light up when your students walk into the room. Do the same when you see their parents.

Just before I had my first baby, I remember a friend telling me that every time I walked in and saw her after time apart, I should light up my eyes and smile with excitement to see her! I did this every single time. And guess what? She used to mirror her enthusiasm straight back to me. I now do this with my dog too! People think I'm weird, but my puppy loves it and responds to it the same way as humans do! Can you see the power in that?

This is the same response you will get from your students, too. Just smile and light up with your students, and they will engage and connect with you from the beginning of class; they will listen to you and want to give you their absolute best.

2. Listening to Understand

When your students are talking to you, listen to understand what they are telling you and don't just listen to respond. Often there can be an underlying reason they are choosing to have the conversation with you. I know it can be tricky in the classroom when you have numerous students trying to tell you about all the things that are happening in their lives. It could be problems at school, issues with their friends or that they are about to go on a holiday to Europe with their family. Whatever it is – *really* listen to them and respond, not only verbally, but also show them through your actions during the lesson that you care enough to acknowledge what they told you about. If you hear or sense a student is feeling deflated, lift their confidence by giving them a compliment or asking them to lead the warm-up. Remember, for many students, dance is their safe and happy place.

3. Empathy and Feeling

Can you remember the feeling you had arriving at class when you were a young dancer? Can you remember the smell of the studio, the perfume your teacher wore and the feeling of new shoes at the beginning of the dance year? I can, and it fills me with such great memories and reminds me of how much I loved going every week.

I also remember how my teacher treated me and how she made me feel. She genuinely loved me and appreciated that I'd chosen to dance at her studio. Teachers – do this! Genuinely love your students and their desire to learn. I often hear teachers complaining about the lack of commitment and respect students have for teachers 'these days'. For sure, things have changed and we need to adapt our teaching accordingly, but there are still many dancers out there who would give up everything to dance. We need to commit ourselves wholeheartedly and without hesitation to ensure they experience the same euphoria as we did growing up in the studio.

4. Gestures and Response

Several years ago, I was at the studio when one of my teachers came out and asked if I'd come in to watch her class do their new dance. Of course, I said yes. I walked into the classroom with a big smile and my eyes lit up showing them I was excited to see them and that I couldn't wait to see what they had been working on. They performed the dance and it was fantastic. Once they finished, I waited for the teacher to say something to her students ... something, anything, would have been okay; like a 'well done, guys' or even a 'thanks'. But she said nothing. I looked at the students. They were staring at her, their bodies leaning in, waiting and wanting any type of feedback or comment, but there was nothing. She gave them *nothing*. After this awkward silence, I chimed in and complimented their performance, noting what I loved and areas I thought they could work on, but essentially I simply *acknowledged* their effort. And, let me tell you, I saw each of the students exhale, drop their shoulders and smile with pride.

Praise every improvement with positivity. It is part of our job to critique, correct and offer constructive feedback for our students to improve and progress, but it doesn't have to be done in a rude, harsh way or – worse still – with silence. It is about acknowledging our students' efforts as well as their results.

5. Voice, Speech and the Words You Choose

The words we use impact our students significantly. Be conscious and deliberate in your conversations and choose your words wisely. Using harsh, judgmental or sarcastic tones will not enhance your students' ability. It will leave them feeling incapable and can result in them losing confidence and emotionally withdrawing. Is that what you wanted when you decided to become a teacher? I don't think so. Depending on the age, ability and experience of your class, your approach, words and tone will differ slightly.

Regardless of these variables, your words should be said with consideration and respect every time. Refer to the list below for some positive phrases and words you can use in class, which will make a big difference as to how the information is received by your students:

- 'It will be ok'
- 'Not a problem'
- 'Sounds great'
- 'Perfect'
- 'You're welcome'
- 'Excellent'
- 'Let's give it a try'
- 'Best thing to do is give the class a go'
- 'What do you love the most about dance/drama/singing?'
- 'Have you danced before? Yes – excellent, you'll love it'; or 'No – that's fine, we have new people starting all the time'

- 'Come in and try the class'
- 'You won't know until you give it a go'
- 'Well done, now let's go through this part again'
- 'Great try, now how about we try it this way'
- 'Hmmm … now that was a good try, but it is not quite how I remember it, so maybe we should go through what we learnt last week another time'
- 'I like that you remembered that part. I think we should run through the other part now'
- 'The choreography we learnt last week was tricky, so it's okay that you are a bit confused. How about you all break up into smaller groups and see if you can remember it together?'
- 'We worked really hard on this last week and you had it looking terrific. Take a moment to work out what we did, and we will re-run it in a couple of minutes.'

Student Connection and Communication

During my years of teaching and interacting with thousands of students in a dance class setting, it became evident to me that each student in my classes fell into one of 5 personality types: excited, contented, attention-seeking, shy or anxious.

Once you identify which personality category each of your students fall into, applying tiny tweaks in how you approach them will make a big difference in how they respond during your class. I'm going to delve a bit deeper now and give you some specific strategies to use.

The 5 Main Personality Types of Dance Students:

Personality Type 1: Excited

These are the students who are excited to be there and almost cannot contain their joy and enthusiasm.

For you, as the teacher:

- Smile, light up your eyes and share your excitement to see them too. This reassures them that their feelings of excitement are welcomed and accepted, and that they will have a great lesson.
- Use their name, and acknowledge and engage with them before the lesson starts.
- Retain their attention with feedback throughout the lesson.
- Place these students near less confident students to help them with their confidence.

Personality Type 2: Contented

These are the students who are content and comfortable and feel no stress being there with you. They feel safe, know what they need to do and do it with a smile. This is ultimately where you should aim for all your students to be.

Some tips with these students are:
- Ensure you acknowledge and engage with them at the beginning of each lesson.
- Smile, light up your eyes and share your excitement to see them too. This reassures them that their feelings are being accepted and acknowledged, and that they will have a great lesson.
- Use their name and compliment them for the great things they do, try and say every lesson.
- Remember that just because they are happy and generally comfortable, doesn't mean they don't still need to be reassured every lesson with positivity and compliments.

Personality Type 3: Attention-Seeking

These are the students who are continually striving for your attention, want to be the centre of attention in class and are often speaking over everyone, including you.

The best way to approach these students is to:
- Acknowledge them as they come into your class.

- Tell them you are happy they are at class and subtly remind them of your expectations around the manners and conduct required from them during the lesson (even for your older students, a quick reminder can trigger their memory from the last time they were in class).
- Gently redirect everyone's attention away from the student if they are jumping in to answer all your questions, by asking someone else for their response or opinion so that all students get an opportunity to speak up.
- Encourage other students in the class to have a voice.

Personality Type 4: Shy

These are the students who are shy and a little uncertain, but trust you enough to be there. They definitely don't want to draw attention to themselves or be singled out to demonstrate.

When this type of student walks into the studio:

- Have a gentle and warm demeanour towards the student (and their parent if they are there).
- Lower the volume and pitch of your voice, so you don't appear over-enthusiastic to see them. Bend down or sit at their level, look them in the eyes, smile and make them feel welcome.
- Reassure them with your body language and words that they are in a safe environment, free from judgement, criticism and embarrassment.
- Ask the student open-ended questions, so they have to respond with more than just a 'yes' or 'no' (e.g. 'Tell me about your day' or 'What is your name?').
- Be consistent with your interactions each week. This will slowly build their confidence as you earn their trust.

Personality Type 5: Anxious

These are the students who have fear in their eyes, and it feels like the last place they want to be is with you in your class. Generally, they will be with their parent at the beginning of each lesson.

I usually find the best way to help these students is to:

- Acknowledge and say hi to the student, being sure to use their name.
- Use a calm and confident tone.
- Approach both parent and student. Engage and say hi to their parent first. Let the student see that their parent trusts you.
- For younger students, don't make eye contact with them at first. You don't want them to feel intimidated.
- Eventually, you will earn their trust and they will feel reassured that they are in a safe place and will have a positive experience.

Your students are individuals and, at times, what works for one won't necessarily work for another. All interactions will be slightly different.

Know that there will be students in your class who you'll find easier to relate to and some you will find more challenging to relate to. Treat all students fairly. It is essential that all students know they are as valued as everyone else in the class. You may naturally find it easier to focus on particular students; however, if you let this show, it will lead to a negative atmosphere in the classroom (and beyond). No one in the class should feel that you favour some students over others.

Avoid a Competitive Atmosphere in Your Classroom

Avoid developing a competitive atmosphere between your students in the classroom. Don't compare students or repeatedly choose the same student to demonstrate. This behaviour can become destructive to the other students who don't get selected. Its adverse effect tends to rub off on parents too, creating problems that extend beyond the classroom. Learn to be creative with your starting positions, dance placements, groups and choreography. Encourage every single student to strive for his or her personal best.

Teaching Students With Learning and Behavioural Challenges and Disabilities

At one stage several years ago, I had a class of children with Down syndrome. There were 12 of these wonderful children in total. They didn't know each other outside of dance, but when they met up once a week at class, they were the best of friends. They encouraged and cheered each other on. What they taught me during those lessons forever made me a much better teacher. I will say with hand on my heart that they are the most beautiful and rewarding students I ever had the privilege to teach. It is an honour to be able to teach every child who wants to learn to dance, especially students with disabilities, behavioural or learning challenges. Although it can sometimes be a little tricky; again, we need to adapt and tweak how we teach to get the best out of them.

In most cases, the parent of a student in your class who has a learning or physical disability or difficulty, or behavioural challenges, will inform you of the details before they start in your class. It is crucial to really listen to the details the parent is telling you. Ask clarifying questions and get clear on what they are saying. Ask more questions if you are unsure (e.g. 'What do you feel would be the best way to handle ...?' or 'How do you think they would go with ...?'). Write down the specifics from the conversation you have with their parents and construct a plan together so you can effectively include and manage this student in your class. Every student is an individual, and one method won't necessarily work with someone else with a similar disability. Stay open-minded, calm and flexible.

And finally, it is crucial that they know they are as valued as any other student in the class; they just hear, learn and process information in a different way. It doesn't have to be overwhelming for you (and most definitely not for them) – you just need to have a plan.

To help you out, I have a PDF, which includes a template of a Disability and Behavioural Plan, as well as a list of strategies to help manage your class. You can check it out here: http://www.

danceteachercentral.com/wp-content/uploads/2018/10/02-Classroom-and-Student-Behaviour-Management-4-Edited.pdf

Discipline in the Classroom

The Oxford English Dictionary defines 'discipline' as:

The practice of training people to obey rules or a code of behaviour …

This principle needs to be taken, adapted and implemented into your classroom.

Over my decades of teaching, these are some common questions I am asked by teachers:

1. How are we able to effectively discipline our students without crossing the line, being too harsh or not being direct enough?

   As the teacher, you need to take responsibility for maintaining positive behaviour in your classes. In many cases, behavioural problems are often a response to boredom or a lack of interest in what is being taught. Another reason could be that you haven't clearly explained your expectations, rules and boundaries, so be sure you are really clear with your students at the beginning of the lesson about what you expect from them and how you want them to achieve that.

   Here is an example of that: 'Today we are going to learn more of our dance. I expect you to listen without talking to your friends while I teach you the choreography. You can practise in groups and individually when I tell you it's time. Write out the choreography in your dance journal, because I expect you to come back next lesson and know what we did, applying all corrections I give you during the lesson. Does that sound okay to you?'

   Now, the chances are that not every student is going to do exactly what you just asked. However, you now have a starting point for a firm discussion if your students start talking or if they don't follow your instructions. You can then remind them of the conversation you had with them at the beginning of the lesson.

2. How can I keep my students engaged during the lesson?
A high-energy class that keeps students constantly moving leaves little opportunity for misbehaviour. A lot of the time, misbehaviour occurs when your attention is pulled away from the class (e.g. if you start searching for music, looking for a pen to mark the roll or talking to a student one-on-one). Once students have enough time to be distracted, it can be tough to bring their focus back to the class. The solution? Don't give them time to act up in the first place!

A tip is not to have students who tend to get distracted or talk a lot to others positioned at the back of the room. Move them to the front of the room so that you can have eye contact with them and engage with them constantly. Separate the talkative students and the ones who have trouble staying focused. Be prepared to go overboard with compliments when these students do something good, because they will respond a lot better with positive comments and feedback. Just be sure that the well-behaved students are not disciplined or disadvantaged for the actions of others.

3. What do I do when I've tried all the tactics and strategies I know, and a student is still misbehaving and distracting the class?
Persistent misbehaviour must be addressed. If a student's behaviour is continually disrupting the class, it is time to speak to their parent or the studio owner. In some circumstances, just talking to their parents will make a difference. If that still doesn't work, I ask the parents to come into the class to witness or control

the behaviour themselves. In extreme but rare cases, I have suggested that the student take a break from dance for a while and maybe try something like football or gymnastics instead!

When you do speak up concerning misbehaviour, be sure your students understand that it's the behaviour you are upset about, not them. Avoid comments that make students feel like failures. If you react to the situation in a respectful way, most students will respond.

Student Communication and Conflict

Personality conflicts will occur, and there will be some people you resonate with and others you don't. When this happens, stay professional, keep smiling and don't take it personally. You will not only notice this with your students, but also their parents, your peers and other teachers as well.

Understand that everyone has different viewpoints and levels of understanding. Add to the mix emotion and exhaustion, and you never know what you may end up dealing with each day!

When it comes to managing people, I have found that prevention is the key. Give your students, parents and peers as much information as possible about your expectations in the first place. That way, you avoid awkward conversations later.

For example:

Classroom expectations:

- Start and finish times
- Whether or not the parent is permitted to observe the lesson
- Photographs and filming rules
- Food and drink requirements
- Uniform and grooming guidelines

Performance and costuming requirements:

- Times
- Dates

- Rehearsals
- What students will need for the day

General communication, behaviour and expectations when at the studio:
- When the best time to talk to the class teacher is
- Who they should speak to if they have any concerns
- What the etiquette in the waiting rooms is

This information puts everyone's mind at ease, reduces frustration, and minimises mistakes and the number of questions that you'll be asked.

Conflict and Confrontation

I don't want to generalise, but I'll assume that you – like most dance teachers I know (myself included) – dislike confrontation.

I remember back to a time at the studio, when I was still quite young and hadn't had much experience dealing with conflict, when a mum came up to me screaming in my face. She was loud and there was an audience of parents sitting in the waiting area, which added to the drama and impact of her performance. As I stood there wide-eyed and in disbelief, my heart started to race, my face started to burn and go bright red, and the sweat built up in my armpits. I can't even remember why this parent was so angry, but I later found out (when she apologised) that she was having dramas in her personal life and I just happened to be the person in the firing line that day.

Maybe you have experienced a similar situation and know what I'm talking about. Or maybe you are lucky enough to have avoided this type of confrontation so far. If and when you are faced with unexpected confrontation, here are my suggestions on how to handle it:
- Take a deep breath and calmly say, 'I am happy to talk to you about this at an appropriate time and place, because here and now is certainly not that. I will contact you to organise a time with you (and a third person) to address your concerns'.

77

- Alternatively, you could say, 'I do not tolerate this kind of behaviour from my students and especially not from their parents. I will speak to you once you have calmed down, in an appropriate place with another person present'.
- Then re-enter the classroom … and breathe.

Calmly dealing with confrontation also sets an example to students of how to behave and it positions you as a teacher who is a positive role model for your students. By responding this way, you maintain your professionalism and grace in front of those who matter (the other parents, students and your peers) – and this is what they will remember.

Thankfully, this is not a regular occurrence (and if it is for you, we need to talk and sort it out quick smart)! The vast majority of your parents and students choose you for the exceptional teacher you are and they will be grateful for that. If you treat them with respect, they will give it back to you.

Be Confident

Your confidence will evolve and – with experience, age and as you progress to mentor and industry leader – you will become more and more sure about the decisions you make.

A few tips I share with new teachers are:

- Don't ever feel intimidated by any of your students. I know sometimes the age gap between you and them won't be all that big, but you need to be confident, well prepared, professional and respectful; however, be aware not to adopt an attitude of superiority.
- There should never be a time where you take your eyes off your class. Continually watch your class and chat to them to keep them engaged. Never turn your back completely.
- Remind your students about being safe and careful. This goes for all ages. Remind the older students of the importance of warming up, stretching and staying hydrated etc. Clearly go

through the rules and, most importantly, explain why we don't engage in certain behaviour.

- Students will test the boundaries in a class. It is essential to react to their behaviour immediately, but calmly and consistently. If you respond to specific actions from one student, you must respond the same way for every student who does the same thing. Sending mixed messages can be just as detrimental as not reacting at all.
- Never overreact. If you lose your composure, you're no longer in control.
- Sometimes you won't have to say a word. A glance or eye contact can send a message that you disapprove of a particular behaviour. Sometimes not saying anything is the best form of discipline.

This brings us to the end of the chapter on Communication and Connection. A lot of these suggestions will be a matter of trial and error. Take a strategy and try it out. If it doesn't work, tweak it a little and then try again. In time, it will become second nature and it will make a significant impact in your classes.

Recap:

Principle 3: Communication and Connection

- Incorporate facial expressions, listening to understand, empathy and feeling, gestures and response, and choose your words carefully to fully engage, connect and convey your message in the classroom
- Genuinely love your students and their desire to learn
- Identify and tweak different strategies to manage the 5 main personality types in your class
- Know that personality conflicts will occur and remember that maintaining your professionalism and grace is what students and parents will remember

Chapter 7
Principle 4: Get Creative In The Classroom

'Create with the heart, build with the mind' – Criss Jami

There is nothing I love more than seeing a teacher raise the 'barre' of expectation and think outside the box, mixing things up and keeping it fresh. A new teacher will generally teach in the way they were taught. Assuming an exceptional teacher taught you, you have an awesome starting point. The challenge is that times have changed. How students take classes has changed, the expectations of parents have changed, and the attitudes and attention spans of many students is now very different from that of several years ago.

While I hear a lot of teachers complain about this (usually those who have been teaching for over 20 years), change is actually a great thing for the industry. Change means growth, innovation and opportunity. Luckily, the industry has you – the talented next generation of teachers – who will embrace these changes and continue to impact and influence the new generation students. And the secret to success here, my friends, is to get creative in all areas of teaching.

I still feel grateful everyday that I was able to set up my dance teaching career and studio. Slowly growing my studio while at school enabled me to step straight into a fully established business the day I finished school.

As I previously mentioned, I love learning. A couple of years after finishing school, I decided it was time to study again. The first subjects I chose were psychology and communications, before I moved into policing. Although the latter choice came as a shock to most people who knew me, the similarities, experiences and what I learned about could also be applied when I was back in the studio.

During my last eight years working as a police officer, I worked in the child protection and sex crimes squad, which is a major crime squad for the state of New South Wales. This opened my eyes to another side of life, which – sadly – is also relevant to the dance industry.

I was a police officer for 13 years while continuing to juggle teaching and managing the studio at the same time. The experience, information and training was so powerful and relevant to teaching and managing my students and staff, that I knew my next step had to be to collate all that knowledge and share it within the dance industry.

When I was training for the police, I vividly remember a safety training exercise where we were taught about different actions and inactions when dealing with the public. These actions or inactions during a situation while on the job could mean the difference between life and death. Funnily enough, I use some examples from this when training my dance teachers.

In policing terms, some of these are:

- 'Relaxing too soon': Just because you think the danger is gone, doesn't mean you can lose focus on the reason you are there.
- 'Making false assumptions': Just because something seems okay, doesn't necessarily mean it is. Don't assume anything.
- 'Failure to watch hands': Don't get distracted by what someone is saying, you always need to be aware of the person's hands, in case they pull out a weapon (in other words, observe a situation, not just what you are being told).
- 'Tunnel vision': Don't focus only on the one thing that seems to be obvious and neglect to see and think outside the box and observe what else is going on.
- 'Complacency': The minute you become complacent on a job, you increase your risk of injury or even death (this is the one I refer to most when I'm teaching).

Now I'm assuming you've put your safe dance practice training into action, so I really hope there is no chance of anyone actually dying in class! However, when I refer to becoming complacent as a teacher, I mean that if a teacher reaches a point where they believe they know everything, they've finished their training for good and don't see the value in continuing their professional development – they are not only doing a disservice to themselves, but to their students as well.

The result of this thinking is that they no longer put any effort or thought into what they are teaching and how they are delivering it to their students. They use the same warm-up exercises, the same progressions, the same music and the same choreography year in and year out. Thankfully no one will die, but the students will become bored and frustrated, and will not progress or continue. I know this because I've seen it happen.

My teachers and I meet up regularly. It is during these meetings where I ask them to share any ideas they might have and chat about new things happening in the industry that we could implement or integrate into our classes. We usually start with the challenges anyone is experiencing or the issues they have identified. Together, we will construct a plan to creatively eliminate the problem. I challenge them to consciously change up the way they run their lessons (e.g. try a different warm-up sequence or change the perspective from where the students stand while learning the choreography).

I have a couple of teachers who I taught when they were young, who then continued training through our assistant teacher training program and are now working as senior teachers at my studios. When I see them start and finish their classes, talk to their students, run the lessons and teach the choreography – I notice they do it exactly how I did it for years. I'd proudly like to add that their retention, growth and progression are excellent – because they are *exceptional* teachers.

In saying that, over the past couple of years, they have identified certain things that are now not working as well as they used to because the way a student learns, listens and responds now is different than it was 20 years ago. This means that I continually have to challenge myself and get creative about tweaking our programming and strategies.

I challenge you to think of ways that you can continually stay creative and fresh while teaching.

Here are some ideas:

- Change up your music regularly. Build a playlist of new release song as well as classics. Also, have a back-up playlist of action songs for younger kids or songs like 'Nut Bush City Limits' for a fun warm-up.
- Bring along some props, stretching or strengthening equipment for variety during skills and technique training.
- Choreograph different warm-up combinations to change it up each lesson.
- Change the direction of where the students stand while you teach.
- Chat with other dance teachers and exchange ideas.
- Read and learn about the latest ideas in teaching, psychology and communication.

Once you come up with some new ideas to try in class, it's time to get creative with your students. This little secret I'm about to share with you is something that not many teachers know. Not because they choose not to do it, but because they don't think on a deeper level about connecting with their students.

Let Your Students Be Part of the Creative Process

By allowing your students to become part of the creative process, it will give them a sense of importance and help develop their confidence, which ultimately strengthens the team atmosphere in the classroom. Ask them about songs that they currently love and current trends that are floating around in the schoolyard. Often we get trapped in a comfortable bubble of what we know and love (sort of like tunnel vision, which – as I said – was part of our police safety training), and it's easy to forget there are so many other options and a huge variety of music, ideas, concepts and stories available to use. For me, I just love the old songs, musicals and the classics like, 'I've Got The Music In Me' and 'River Deep Mountain High'.

Personally, I find it hard to resonate with new release songs, not to mention the fact that it can be a bit tricky with a lot of the lyrics and connotations being too inappropriate to use. However, I am self-aware enough to know that, in order to help deepen the connection with my students, I need to include the music and songs that this generation of students know and love. Another bonus of this generation is that we have an abundance of information, music choices and inspiration right at our very fingertips. There is no excuse for you to become complacent when the options are endless.

Incorporate fun activities and creative exercises into your lessons. Not only will this help your students learn, grow and retain technique and chore, but they will also love coming to dance and be eager to come back the following week. Try breaking your class into groups, putting a song on and asking them to choreograph 32 counts. Get each group to show the rest of the class and, you never know, you may even be able to incorporate some of it into a routine – win/win.

Give your students some responsibilities. Let them know they are responsible for leading a particular section of the warm-up, welcoming a new student or even just the fact they are expected to come back to class knowing the chore because they are part of a team and they shouldn't let the team down. This is going to strengthen their self-worth and confidence and, hopefully, they'll return the next lesson knowing the chore!

I have a PDF with some warm-up and programming ideas, which you may find helpful. You can find it here: http://www.danceteachercentral.com/wp-content/uploads/2017/10/WARM-UPS-PROGRAMMING-CLASS-IDEAS-FOR-2-8YRS.pdf

Talk honestly and openly with your students. Share your ideas and the concepts of what you are planning. If you have the opportunity, allocate some time to sit with them and talk them through your thoughts. Explain your vision, music choice, costumes and the props you may use. As you talk them through it, watch their eyes and facial expressions. You'll see them start to visualise what you are describing. Their heads will begin to nod slightly in agreement as they absorb the information you are telling them and you'll see their brains start to tick over and come up with ideas to contribute and build on.

I realise that, in many cases, their views are not going to align with yours, but the fact you give them the feeling of sharing and adding to the original idea will provide them with a sense of accomplishment and achievement. (And sometimes, just sometimes, one of them will come up with a golden idea that you end up using!)

Get Creative With the Way You Position Your Students

Get creative with the way you position your students for their routines. I've previously talked about how you're going to love working with and teaching some of your students and others not so much, and how it's important not to show favouritism to any one student. There will always be one or two in the class who put in 100 per cent each lesson, know the chore each week and shine on stage. It's tempting to place them front and centre of every routine because they are mostly carrying the rest of the group. However, in order for everyone in your class to feel equal and valued, you shouldn't have the same student spotlighted every time.

Over the years, I have thought of ways to cleverly position my students so that everyone, regardless of their level of skill or ability, has an opportunity to shine. Below is a strategic plan to position students so that the same dancers are not centre front each time, but the routines still look amazing and it's fair for everyone.

Before you go through this process, you need to have planned out how you are going to start the dance. Have an idea of who you want to start where, so that when you are applying these strategies it will work in your favour.

Creativity Strategy 1: Clever Start Chore

You need to have a strong start to any routine, which is why we always want our strongest dancers in the front position every time … but what if you started your routine with a different format? To allow some of your weaker dancers to begin in the front, you could have several groups of dancers spread around the stage (possibly kneeling), with those students at the front of their group performing an effective arm combo or strong but more simplified chore so they nail it. Then, after the opening section, arrange your dancers so the stronger ones move forward for the first section.

Creative Strategy 2: Height Order

Ask your students to stand in one line from shortest to tallest. Depending on your start plan, start at one end of that line and send each dancer either to different parts of the classroom or a particular spot of your planned formation. Try and fill your configuration from the back of the stage to the front or from one side to the other, as opposed to starting front centre. Place your students in what appears to be random order, while what you are actually doing is balancing out your stronger and weaker dancers.

Creative Strategy 3: Number Head Count

Ask your students to stand in a group and tap them on the head or shoulder as you give each of them a number (e.g. 1, 2 or 3). Appear to do this randomly within the group, but – depending on your start plan and knowing roughly where you want each of your students to be positioned – be deliberate in which number you give them. Know that all 1s are going to start stage right, all 2s are going to make a line across the back of the stage and all 3s will be the group that travels to the front.

Creative Strategy 4: Mixed Strength Groups

Place your students into groups. Mix the group up with a combination of the stronger and weaker dancers. When you work out the positioning within the individual groups, you can strategically place each dancer according to their ability. Dancers can be in several lines or in a group offset to the dancers in front and you can change up those positions with your choreography.

These 4 strategies are clever ways to get you started.

Another innovative twist when positioning your students is to not always group your stronger dancers with each other and your weaker dancers with each other. Mix them together and you'll see the weaker students work extra hard and strive to improve.

A few years ago, I had a teacher who repeatedly and excessively favoured the stronger dancers in his routines. He would start everyone on together at the beginning of a dance, then have the weaker dancers go off stage to showcase the stronger dancers for an extended period of the dance. They would then go off stage, and the weaker dancers would return. He would have them perform very basic (and not very creative) chore for a short time, only to return the stronger group back on the stage, positioned to finish the routine front and centre, while the weaker dancers were off to the back and sides. He had the same dancers in these groups for every single routine.

Eventually, one of the girls came to me and said that she and the others in her group 'are starting to feel like back-up dancers' and that the teacher was making it very obvious that he didn't really care or put any time or thought into them. 'He only focuses on the great dancers,' she said. It broke my heart to hear. This girl had been dancing with me for 11 years and loved it so much. My studio is not about the dancing hierarchy at all. My teachers know that everyone needs to feel included and as important as each other. Needless to say, he is no longer with us as he was unable to think outside the box and creatively change the way he taught.

Some ideas on being creative and inclusive could be to:

- Teach chore to the group as a whole and get them to break into groups themselves to demonstrate the routine to each other.

- Get your students to make up some chore and teach it to each other.
- Ask your students to run a warm-up, so each student has to think of an exercise and lead the class.
- Schedule in time for improvisation during the class.

Be Creative With How You Deliver Corrections

It is essential for dance teachers to give feedback and corrections to students. If we didn't do that, we would be doing a disservice to our students. Without this feedback, students wouldn't correctly progress. Worse still, they could continue through their dance years risking long-term injury or joint damage because they weren't manipulated or shown correct body placement and technique. *But* – and this is a big but – there are many creative ways to give feedback, offer correction and address issues that come up, which are far more effective than the typical 'old school' (or as I like to refer to it as – the 'Dance Mom's') way of delivering corrections.

There will never be a time or place where it is appropriate to belittle or shame a student. It doesn't matter what has occurred or what they may have done. I'm not saying to ignore the issue or make light of anything that may be serious, but shaming or condescending a student will achieve nothing and not move you any closer to the outcome you were hoping for.

Some of the suggestions below offer an alternate and inventive way to communicate this with your students.

Address the Issue or Correction as a Group

Okay, so ... you've spent a lot of time with little 'Sophie' correcting her turnout and posture when performing her fouetté turns. You see her practising, but she is still not nailing it. It is frustrating for you because you don't know what else to try. You've explained how to do it as clearly as possible and demonstrated it for her several times. It's not from a lack of trying on Sophie's part. She really is doing her best. If you continue to point out to Sophie every lesson that she is still not turning out properly, she will start to feel like a failure, begin to withdraw and eventually give up. In instances like this, a good tactic is to address the issue or correction as a group, rather than honing in on one particular student. Teach the whole class different turnout exercises and progressions, and give the entire class specific steps and techniques to practise at home, even though it is mainly for Sophie's benefit. This way, she won't be able to identify that she is the only one still yet to master the step.

Ask Questions

You've identified 'Charlotte' in your class is still struggling with a particular part of the routine. It's usually the less confident dancers who take a little longer to get the chore. You've spent a fair amount of class time going over it already, but she is still struggling.

Ask questions to the class as a way to fix this section of the dance (e.g. stand in front of your class and break down each part of that particular section of the dance). Ask the class, 'When we put our arm out to the side, do we have our fingers opened or hand clenched in a fist?' Let them do the step with you, giving the answer as they do. Then say, 'Yes, the hand is clenched and in a fist – now let's practise that with more strength and power ... Good, let's try it again even stronger this time'.

By doing this, you are breaking down and cleaning up the routine, giving a slower and more precise explanation for Charlotte and anyone else in the class who hasn't quite got it yet, without singling out one particular student.

Praise the Effort

Another creative tactic is to praise the effort of each of your students. Highlight positive behaviour and excellent listening, and thank those who are trying really hard. If there is one student who isn't focused, continually chatting or distracting the class, say to the class as a whole, 'I love how hard a lot of you are trying today,' or 'Thank you to those who are listening well today. It certainly makes my job of teaching you our new dance fun and easy when you are paying attention'. My all-time favourite, especially for the older students, is, 'You are now at the top end of the studio. You are a role model and the younger dancers are looking up to you. Make sure you show them exactly how to behave, speak and respect each other'. This strategy will work nine times out of 10, but – if not – keep reading on for another idea.

Use Eye Contact and Empathy

It's important to remember that your students will have a level of self-awareness. Once they reach a certain age, they become aware that they may not be the strongest dancer in the class or that they may be less fit than others. You, as the teacher, also need to be aware of this and respond in a creative way that will not shatter their confidence or make them feel worthless. Use eye contact and empathy to discreetly reassure them. This way you aren't bringing unwanted attention to them, but they are still being encouraged.

On the flip side, you will also have students who are continually trying to be the centre of attention and talking over others in the class. Before losing your patience, stop for a moment to ask yourself, '*Why* is this student acting in such a way?' There is a good chance they actually *lack* self-confidence (contrary to their actions). Ask yourself what could be a skilful way to settle them down so they are less distracting for the rest of the class, thereby making the class flow better for you. I find that by giving these students responsibilities or tasks (such as helping any new students who need to catch up on the chore or filling up my water bottle) gives them something to focus their energy into and also helps them to feel worthy and important.

Take Them Aside and Have a Chat

Say you've tried all the other options and 'Abbie' is still not getting it. You've addressed the group, trying to take the focus off her so she doesn't feel like she's letting everyone down or that you are continually correcting her for that particular part of the dance. You've used indirect tactics such as asking everyone to break into groups and practise that specific section of the routine, and asking questions of the class as a whole, but it's still not working. The next thing to try is to speak to Abbie directly, but it is important you take her aside or do it when no one else in the class is paying attention or can hear what you say.

Sometimes a student will need to hear your feedback clearly and directly. You still must not belittle them, shame them or make them feel worthless. Instead, offer some clarification, suggestions to help improve the situation and the expectation of what you want from them next time you see them. Again, talk to them respectfully, knowing that they are probably going to be a bit embarrassed. It can be a little awkward at times, but this is part of our job and responsibility to give our best to our students.

What Do You Do if Nothing Works?

Sometimes, no matter what we do, it still doesn't produce the desired outcome. We do have our limits and we can't always work miracles. There are times when we just have to accept that we don't have a solution to every single problem we face.

The more years of teaching experience you have, the more solutions you'll have in your repertoire that can solve *almost* every problem or help in *nearly* every situation. Only time will give you this knowledge and expertise.

It's not hard to come up with creative ideas, it just takes a bit of time and a little effort to think and act from a new perspective. The benefits of doing so are significant. The connection will be heightened with your students and you will begin to see them soar.

Recap:
Principle 4: Get Creative in the Classroom

- Get creative: Stay fresh, don't get complacent and remember to think outside the norm
- Let your students be part of the creative process
- Get creative with how to deliver feedback and corrections

Chapter 8

Principle 5: Professional and Personal Development

Create a life that feels good on the inside, not one that just looks good on the outside.

Several years ago, I sat with my husband in our kitchen and chatted to him about the fact I wanted to change the direction of my business. My studio was running smoothly. I had a dedicated, passionate and reliable team of teachers. But my focus had changed from teaching my students to dance to training my teachers to teach.

I had a real calling in my heart to do this, which meant I had to pivot so I could step into the next stage of my career. Not only was this going to be a financial risk, but also an enormous time commitment, requiring time away from my family and friends while I put my head down and made this dream viable. I had new things to learn, courses to do and I also had to learn a 'new language' within the industry.

This decision was undoubtedly going to impact my family in some way, but I also knew how this could radically influence and change the lives of many other dance teachers and educators across the world. I knew I was destined for bigger and better things, and that now was the right season of my life to make it happen. It required me to step out of my comfort zone, push my boundaries and challenge what I thought I already knew.

The opportunities available to all of us these days are endless. There is an abundance of information at our fingertips and, honestly, if you have the dream and the inner drive to do something – you *can* make it happen.

If you are similar to the hundreds of dance teachers I have the privilege of engaging with, then you will have a desire to do something more. You will have a dream and a spark in your heart to share your passion and love for dance with the world.

Maybe you choose to tell others, or perhaps it just sits quietly in your heart because you're afraid of the unknown. Possibly it's the fear of being vulnerable, being judged, or the repercussions you could face if you do choose to pivot. But … if it's there, I think it's there for a reason, and that you are capable of accomplishing your dream.

Just take one step at a time, even if it's a small one. Keep heading in the direction of your dreams and watch it all unfold.

Stop comparing yourself to others, stop worrying about what others will think, stop trying to exceed their expectations; just stay true to yourself and your dream, and you will astound yourself with what you can achieve. Be the best version of *you*, not who you think others want you to be. You do you! If you live your best life, you will change the lives of all those around you … and isn't that what it's truly all about?

Look at your career in seasons. There are going to be seasons of growth, seasons of change, seasons of smooth sailing and seasons of unrest. The secret is not to let the season throw you off course. Assess the season you are in and determine whether you need to pivot, rest or power through.

So … go with confidence and courage and make it happen. You've got this!

Don't be disheartened with the timing of things coming to fruition. Time is a funny thing. I find, once we've made up our mind to start chasing that dream, we want it straight away – like *right now*! However, it usually doesn't work like that and it's at that point where you have to stay laser-focused and keep taking those small steps every day to get there. Everything will align when the time is right. When you do finally arrive at your destination, you will realise that the timing was perfect all along.

There are areas in your life you can control and areas you can't; however, there is great power in identifying the parts you can control and making them work for you, not against you. As you can probably tell after reading this book, I love structure and a good plan!

I have discovered the value of focusing on the following 3 key areas. Managing these things has kept me accountable, on track and moving forward. I'm going to talk you through them below.

The 3 key areas you need to manage:

1. Your environment: Manage the external things around you
2. Yourself: Manage habits to better your health and body
3. Beyond yourself: Make conscious and intentional decisions that affect you mentally and emotionally

Let's start with things you can manage surrounding you. These are the physical things you manage externally.

1. Your Environment: Manage the External Things Around You

- Have a positive morning routine
- Be consistent
- De-clutter your life
- Give to others

Have a Positive Morning Routine

How you start your day will set the tone for the rest of your day. Let me say that again, so I can be sure you read it! How you *start* your day will set the tone for the rest of your day.

Get clear on your intentions for the day ahead. Have a plan. What do you *need* to do? What do you *want* to do? Schedule it in, so you are consciously taking small steps to reach your goals.

Try starting your day just by making your bed. At least that can be counted as one win for the day, just in case the wheels fall off later! Breathe, meditate or journal your thoughts if that's for you. Just take a couple of minutes to remind yourself of the dream you are working towards – that thing on your heart that is going to change the lives of the people around you.

In Chapter 5, I wrote a list of things you could include as part of your daily routine. Head back there if you are looking for some ideas.

Be Consistent

I look at consistency as setting the wheels in motion to keep your momentum rolling. If you truly want the ability to move forward, it's the small things you do every day that will shape your life and set you up for success.

Apply consistency across all areas of your life. Remember, you are a package deal. Not only do you want consistency for growing your career, but also think about applying it to your relationships, diet and exercise.

Getting yourself into a positive health cycle will allow you to focus, get clarity and have energy to power through your day, ultimately bringing you closer to your goals and dreams.

De-Clutter Your Life

When you remove the noise, the negativity and the clutter from around you, you will experience a feeling of space inside your mind, your environment and your career. When you de-clutter your life, you feel a weight begin lifting off your shoulders. Everything feels easier, lighter and clearer for you to start fresh.

The best place to start is by unfollowing people on social media who annoy or frustrate you, or no longer add value to your life. No one has time for that. My husband always says, 'If it makes you screw your face up or raises your heart rate with frustration or anxiety, then get rid of it.' Unsubscribe from emails that no longer serve you well.

Clear out your wardrobe, bathroom vanity and any cupboards, rooms and areas you spend time in, as this will give you more space and energy to use to create.

Once you have cleared the space, the opportunity for new and exciting things will start to emerge. You will feel a sense of calm and control, making way for bigger and better things. Try it – it will change your life!

Give to Others

To finish off with the external areas of your life, I want to talk about giving to others. As teachers, it is in our psyche to want to help out others and give back.

Think back to a time when you were given some advice or a helping hand with something. Look out for opportunities where you can do that for others. I'm not only talking about your students, but also think about donating or offering your time to charities that resonate with you and align with your values.

Get into the cycle of giving to others with no expectation of receiving anything in return. There is no better feeling.

2. Yourself: Manage Habits to Better Your Health and Body

- Health
- Awareness
- Healthy habits
- Mentor or role model

Health

I'm not in favour of the pressure put on women and girls to be really slim. Rather, I am talking about giving your body and mind the optimum chance to function at its highest level and simply feeling great on the inside.

Nutritious food that boosts your energy, movement that releases your endorphins (the happy chemicals in your body) and reduces your levels of cortisol (the stress chemicals in your body), adequate sleep and rest to enable your body to recover and repair itself, are all essential when it comes to your health.

For you to best handle stress and anxiety, you need to find a beautiful balance (it's important to note, this isn't an equally split balance). You have to do the work, enjoy the good stuff and enjoy the company of good people who build you up and don't drain the life out of you.

Awareness

I've spoken a lot about awareness throughout this book and, hopefully, I've made it clear to you how important awareness is for your personal and professional growth and success. Awareness gives you clarity, allowing you to extend and challenge yourself.

You hear from various coaches, mentors and those 'in the know', comments such as: 'Give 100 per cent, strive for perfection and win at all costs'.

Let me explain my alternate theory:

- The 80 per cent rule

So, what exactly is the 80 per cent rule and how does it affect my awareness?

Remember back to being at school ... not kindergarten or primary school, but high school. Remember when you did exams that you actually had to study for – 3 Unit Maths, English, Chemistry – where 80 per cent was an achievable result; however, you needed to study and apply yourself if you wanted to achieve that result. 80 per cent requires a commitment to achieve. Most mere mortals don't just pull 80 per cent from sheer genetic superiority!

So, keep that thought in mind because we will come back to it.

In our lives we are constantly juggling all the various components to live a happy and healthy existence. If you really break it down, you will find that life has many more components than you may immediately realise. Let's look at some of the basics: relationships, health, finances, career – these are some of the more obvious ones. Some would think that if they have these different areas in order, they are well on their way to living a happy and fulfilling life.

However, if you really break them down further, the list is much more extensive than that. Let me list a few, which you can group under the categories above: physical health, diet, mental health, spiritual health, skin health, cash flow, income, wealth, future wealth, investments, marriage, relationships with your children, friendships, trust, work-related education, tertiary education, life-related education, health education, finance education etc.

My theory is that you cannot be good at everything. But, likewise, you should not be bad at everything (or anything, for that matter). The overall aim is to have balance across all areas, so you can lead a quality and happy existence for you and those close to you.

Healthy Habits

Developing healthy habits is another way to keep you accountable. Habits are conscious and deliberate actions that keep you moving forward towards your dreams. This could be exercising regularly or limiting your social media usage by only checking at set times during the day.

A 3-step pattern to help you achieve in forming good habits are:

1. Reminder: The trigger that initiates the behaviour. This could be an alarm you set on your phone or a note you leave on your mirror. Every time you hear or see it, it reminds you to act or respond.

2. Routine: The behaviour itself; the action you take. The reminder isn't enough. You have to consciously get up and take action.

3. Reward: The benefit you gain from doing the behaviour. The feeling, reward and progress are the result of you taking action.

Set reminders or have a checklist nearby, if you need to, to trigger your healthy habits every day.

Mentor or Role Model

Find yourself a positive mentor or role model. As I write this, it's as though I can hear you saying, 'I don't have the money to be able to do that'! Well … guess what? You don't have to pay for it! Two of my favourite mentors are Oprah and Tony Robbins. Granted, they don't have the slightest idea who I am; however, if you ask me – we've been business besties for years!

I watch and listen to their advice and teachings, and apply them in my life, drawing on their wisdom and experience to better myself.

Find that person for you or hang out with people who are going to lift you up and make you a better version of yourself.

3. Beyond Yourself: Make Conscious and Intentional Decisions That Affect You Mentally, Emotionally and Spiritually

- Ambition
- Intention
- Curiosity
- Motivation

Ambition

Ambition gives you the drive and determination to continue to strive forward and reach your dreams.

Don't let anyone crush your ambition. It requires discipline and accountability to manage it well. A little word of advice I'm going to offer here is to be mindful of the 80 per cent rule that I explained earlier. Sometimes a person's ambition leads them to giving 100 per cent towards a particular goal, at the expense of all others. You need to manage your ambition without neglecting the other areas of your life that are just as important.

Intention

An intention is an idea that you plan to carry out. Your goals, purpose and aims make up your intention. There is power in having clear intentions. Again, it is going to keep you on track to heading towards your dreams.

Having intention is about self-integrity and honesty. Be purpose-driven with your intentions. The trick is that you have to do the work. You have to action and follow through on your intention to make it work for you.

Curiosity

Always question 'why?' and check if there is a quicker, better or more efficient way to do things. Ask people you know and trust if you aren't sure or don't understand why they said or did something.

The desire to want to know more is so essential for your success. It is something that should be nurtured and developed; develop a keen interest in extending your knowledge. Being actively interested and genuinely wanting to know more about a topic provides more significant opportunities and experiences, so never be afraid to ask more questions or delve deeper to find answers.

Motivation

Motivation is the reason for doing something or behaving in a particular way. Everyone's idea and perception of motivation will differ, so you need to identify what motivation means for you.

Many variables will impact an individual's motivation level (e.g. they may be tired, sick or working to a deadline). All of these factors will impact on motivation.

When you assess your motivation, you need to ask yourself: What drives your enthusiasm for doing something? What is the need? What is the reason you are doing it? How willing are you to implement it?

Motivation gets the momentum started … so push on and keep going. The moment you begin to lose your motivation, you need to fall back on the good habits you've established, so you continue to be consistent while your motivation begins building up again. Can you see how it all works together?

Start by believing in yourself and knowing that you are valuable, worthwhile and capable.

Luck! What's That?

It makes me giggle when people say to me, 'You're so lucky to have what you have' or 'You're so lucky to be where you are'. The truth of the matter is that luck doesn't have much to do with it at all. What I have and where I am, is a direct result of many years of consistent work, planning, awareness, good habits and not allowing myself to make excuses. It is a result of putting my head down and doing the work; checking in on my goals, dreams and balance to ensure my intentions are always positive, and that I consciously ask questions to learn as much as I can so I continue to grow. See? Not much luck involved. I just made sure I consistently did the work.

But you know you can do it too, right? It really is as simple as following the advice in this chapter. Go back and re-read, adjust and tweak it to make it work for you. These are the small steps I talk about. Doing these little things every day is what will make you exceptional, no matter what stage of the teacher evolution you're at.

So … no more excuses – just *start*.

Recap:

Principle 5: Professional and Personal Development

- Start with the actions that influence the environment surrounding you: Have a positive morning routine, be consistent, de-clutter and give to others.

- Work on habits, actions and emotions within yourself: Take control of your health, awareness and habits, don't make excuses and find yourself a great mentor or role model.
- Delve deep inside your mind and heart and focus on practices, actions and emotions that are beyond yourself: Ambition, intention, growth, curiosity and motivation.

Chapter 9
Becoming an Industry Leader

Becoming an industry leader means that you not only teach,
you take a leadership role in the industry.

To become an industry leader, you need to be the type of master teacher who enables your students to feel confident and empowered, someone who is excited to see them soar and someone who encourages them to flourish and reach their full potential.

Sometimes this will mean encouraging a student to move on from your studio to work with another teacher who can stretch them to their full capacity. If needed, you will have the humility and honesty to say to a student or parent, 'I've taken you up to this point and I can't take you any further. If you want to forge a career in dance, I'm going to recommend you go to (particular studio) and be taught by (specific teacher).' This is *true* leadership. It is about having students' best interest at heart and their career at the forefront of your mind, even if it means advising them that the best course of action may in fact be to continue on with a different studio.

When you're ready to step up to the final level and join the ranks of industry leader, you're ready to take on the challenge of becoming someone with something to say in the field of dance. By this stage of your career, you've worked really hard and you've moved through the earlier 3 stages of evolution: student teacher, teacher and mentor. Another sign you know you've reached this stage is when you sense you're also the type of teacher or mentor who wants to extend your reach beyond your own studio to take an active leadership role in the wider world of dance. This means your vision reaches out into the dance industry as a whole. It means stepping out beyond your local and regional areas – or even your nation – to join forces with other industry leaders worldwide.

Industry leaders have a shared vision to extend the reach of dance and increase the level of excellence in the dance teaching profession. By becoming an influential dance industry leader, it means that you not only teach, but you also become actively involved in the industry from a leadership perspective.

Making the decision to step forward as someone who wants to say more, do more and share more in this industry is one thing, but actively making it happen is another. In order to become an industry leader, you will have developed to a high level in your teaching and mentoring, and you will have gained true mastery in these areas.

The Oxford English Dictionary defines the word 'mastery' as:

Comprehensive knowledge or skill in a particular subject or activity.

To achieve mastery requires you to have self-discipline, motivation and focus on the processes and habits of learning every day so that you can excel at something you are passionate about and dedicated to. As well as developing to the mastery level in your teaching, you will have also had an urge to play a bigger game, be more visible and shine a light on something you see as important in the dance industry. This gives you the insight you need to become an industry leader.

Ask yourself these questions, as they'll help you discover whether you're ready to step into industry leadership:

- As a teacher, do you operate beyond what you understand to be usual and ordinary?
- Are you remarkable when it comes to delivering to your students?
- Are you developing a state of mastery both inside and outside of the studio?

- Are you dedicated to developing and introducing positive change in the industry as a whole?
- Are you committed to developing the next generation of industry leaders?

If you answered 'yes' to these questions, then you're well on your way to stepping into your role as an industry leader.

Your students are the future of the dance industry. They are the future singers, dancers and actors of the performing arts. They are also the future passionate participants and spectators in the world of dance. They may or may not end up working in the industry, but one thing is for sure: you – as their dance educator – have the power, responsibility and influence to be able to help them grow into the next generation of confident and creative adults.

Positioning Yourself as a Leader in the Dance Industry

What can you do to position yourself as an industry leader?

- Innovate: Be creative and innovative and move the industry forward.
- Speak: Speak at events and conferences about what matters for students and teachers.
- Network: Network and truly connect with other dance studio owners and teachers who share similar values.
- Take a stand: Take a stand for what you believe in with regards to the future of dance.
- Write: Write blogs, books and articles about the dance industry and the vision you have for it.
- Podcast: Appear on podcasts or have your own podcast so you can share through conversation and discussion the challenges and trends the dance industry faces.
- Video: Make videos discussing the trends you see currently, what you think would make the industry stronger and what you see in terms of possibilities for the industry.

- Intellectual Property: Build up your Intellectual Property based on your expertise.

Innovate

To become an industry leader, you need to have creative ideas for innovation in this industry so that it moves forward. Industries only move forward and become better, stronger and more exciting if the people within them lead with their ideas. These ideas then have to be shared with as many people in the industry as possible and discussed with people who have the power to make changes.

To be able to have creative ideas, it's important to keep up with the latest changes and ideas in the industry. This means reading dance magazines, books and websites, and it also means attending conferences and professional development seminars that bring industry leaders, teachers and dancers together for discussions and debate.

Part of being a leader in any capacity is to have a vision for the people you are leading. In the dance industry, it is no different. As an industry leader, you need to have new and innovative ideas in teaching, studio management, choreography, marketing, leadership and all other aspects of dance. These fresh ideas get people talking and instigate discussions about how to propel the industry forward, which is what being an industry leader is all about.

Speak

There are events and conferences happening all the time in your local and regional areas, as well as nationally and internationally. Attending events and conferences is great but, to truly be seen as a leader, you need to take the next step and be *speaking* at these events. This positions you as a presenter – as someone who has something to say.

When you speak, you need to be telling an important message, which adds to the knowledge and skills that people already have. Dance industry leaders add value. They don't just repeat what has already been said. It isn't a case of just getting in front of more and more people; it's about getting in front of people and having something new to say, which is useful and valuable to the industry.

You'll need to be proactive in finding out where events and conferences are happening and then apply to be a speaker. Think about a new and exciting idea or discovery that you could talk about, which moves the dance industry, or your area of dance, forward in some way. Then craft a really interesting talk that's not just general in nature, but that suits your particular audience. Watching other top speakers on video, doing a course or joining a group that teaches public speaking skills will elevate your presenting ability. This dramatically helps you in your ability to give talks that are high quality and memorable.

Network

Networking is about becoming well connected. It's about knowing lots of people and connecting with them regularly. It is hard to become a leader in an industry if you're isolated or you only interact with a few people. Part of having an influence in an industry is meeting and knowing a wide range of people from all parts of the dance industry. This means you are bouncing a lot of ideas around, as well as hearing a lot of news and fresh ideas from others.

When you have a large network, it means you are much more likely to get offered opportunities to be part of group projects, be on committees or panels, or to give your opinion. All these things contribute to you becoming a trusted person who is seen to know a lot of people and have a lot of knowledge. It contributes to you being recognised as an industry leader.

Take a Stand

As an industry leader, you will be willing to take a stand, to politely voice your opinion or be forthcoming about what you believe in when it comes to dance education. You will be prepared to talk about your ideas on the future of dance. Being willing to risk people seeing you as outspoken to stand up for what you believe in is part of showing leadership. If you do have something controversial to say, you also have the understanding that – with that – comes responsibility. You may suffer backlash, people may respond to you negatively and you may even have to seek legal advice. However, as someone who wants to lead from the frontline, this is something you may have to navigate if you decide you really want to (or, importantly – feel you need to) take a stand on an issue.

Write

Writing is really effective when it comes to getting your voice heard and positioning yourself as a leader. Writing a regular, up-to-the-minute blog gives you an opportunity to write about current issues and ideas in dance.

Articles offer an opportunity for you to explore an idea in more detail. Dance and performing arts magazines, in general, are places that industry leaders want to be seen. Articles don't have to be written as regularly as blog posts, but it is a good idea to be consistent. When you approach a magazine or website and pitch ideas for articles, you could propose a series of three articles that focus on particular topics under a certain theme.

Aim for specificity, rather than being general in what you say. Choose something in the industry that you feel strongly about or have a new idea for and focus on that. Be specific in what you write about and the details you provide. General information will not position you as a leader. New ideas and focus will.

When readers see your name cited as the author of articles, this starts to position you as an expert.

Podcast

Podcasting is fast becoming one of the most popular ways for people to consume information. The reason for this is that they can listen on the run (quite literally), but also while driving, waiting in line or even while doing the laundry! When people hear you being interviewed, they learn a lot about your ideas and they start to understand how much knowledge you have. They will begin to see you as a serious player in the industry.

When you are interviewed, focus on something specific to talk about rather than keeping it generic. Get people thinking so that after they've listened to you, they are left with something different, something to share with others or something that gets them thinking.

Video

Appearing on camera is a powerful way of being seen as an expert and a leader. The more you are seen and heard, the more you will move towards industry leader status. Video is one of the most important parts of your plan when you want to step into the spotlight and become an industry leader, and that's because it's visual. People love being able to relate to others by seeing them. They will connect with you in a deeper way by observing the way you interact and how you move and respond to things. Becoming comfortable in front of the camera will be one of your secret weapons when it comes to stepping forward in this industry.

Intellectual Property

Intellectual Property (IP) refers to all your original creations that are protected by copyright. It includes things such as blog posts, articles, books, lesson plans, study guides, manuals – anything that you've written or constructed. It also includes trademarks, patents and designs. This book you're reading is part of my suite of IP, and so to is the rest of the training and other materials I have created.

Your IP is constructed from your own ideas, thoughts and knowledge. It is what makes you original, an expert and a thought leader in the dance industry. It is vital to build up your IP if you want to become an industry leader, so that people will be able to find out what you know, what you think and what your ideas are. IP development is a core foundation of becoming a leader in the dance industry.

Being an Industry Leader Inspires the Next Generation

Over the years, I've looked deeply at how our industry works, how extraordinary teachers are made and how true transformation happens in the studio for our students. As you step forward to lead, you will empower and inspire the next generation. Sometimes you may feel unsure and lack confidence, even when you know aspiring teachers are looking towards you for guidance and inspiration. It is helpful to focus on your career as a whole, not just the end goal. Look at the big picture and always do more than just motivate – *show* them why they're learning something and *share* with them how to execute it.

Dance teaching, education, mentoring and leading is a lifelong journey for you, personally. The seasons will come and go – some will be good, others not so good – and you will need to stay courageous and honest to who you are and the difference you are making to those around you. Be a role model for change. Don't just challenge people to change – show them how to make effective change in their lives. Continue growing, learning and developing every day. Each one of your goals makes up only one part of the whole journey, so don't stop when you reach a particular goal – celebrate it, then set your next one. Life is a journey, not just a destination. It's *during* the process that you become a true master and an industry leader. Your passion will help you endure the distance, while you work in a career serving others.

Conclusion

Never stop learning.

A career in dance is built on a lifelong love for this art form and this industry. We start as dance students and – as we progress, learn and study – we may decide to have a professional career as a dancer or we may decide to move into a career as a dance teacher, educator, choreographer, examiner or adjudicator (or all of the above)!

If you take the road of the dance teacher, you will move through the 4 Stages of Dance Teacher Evolution – from student teacher, teacher, mentor to industry leader – and throughout your career you will work towards being better and better at what you do.

When it comes to being truly great at your craft, you will focus on the 5 Principles of Mastery we've discussed in this book. The beauty of this is that you don't stop – even when you have reached the position of industry leader, there is continual development of those principles, so that your mastery of dance teaching, mentorship and leadership becomes more and more refined.

In conclusion, I'm recapping what sits at the core of this book. That is: the understanding of the 4 Stages of Dance Teacher Evolution, as well as the knowledge of the 5 Principles of Mastery.

The 4 Stages of Dance Teacher Evolution

Stage 1: Student Teacher

This is your *training stage*. During this stage you are learning how to teach, so you need to:
- Study the technical training of dance
- Experience and learn as many different genres as you can
- Observe others – as many different teachers and mentors as possible
- Offer your time
- Develop your reputation
- Know your true worth
- Open your mind and never stop learning

Stage 2: Teacher

This stage is about *working for others*. During this stage you need to:
- Put your training into practice
- Focus on connection
- Know the 5 main personalities in the classroom and what strategies to use
- Effectively plan and prepare
- Understand and implement exceptional communication
- Develop trust and learn how to gain mutual respect
- Keep your kids safe

Stage 3: Mentor

This stage is when you are *responsible for others* and *work for yourself*. During this stage you need to:
- Develop your leadership skills
- Train and guide other teachers – practical and theoretical
- Share your knowledge and experiences
- Give time to less experienced teachers
- Share more than just dance skills
- Nurture your students, as well as younger teachers

- Embrace a wider personal approach

Stage 4: Industry Leader

This stage is where you transition to *work for all*. During this stage you will develop the foundations of becoming an industry leader by:

- Completing the hours required to achieve a level of mastery
- Continuing to deliver and receive higher-level training
- Becoming a thought leader, influencer or changer in the industry
- Earning respect as an authority in the industry
- Responding and acting consciously to people and events
- Knowing who you are and who you are not
- Having a mindset of giving, helping and making a change for the better

The 5 Principles of Mastery

Principle 1: Awareness
Principle 2: Planning and preparation
Principle 3: Connection and communication
Principle 4: Creativity in the classroom
Principle 5: Professional and personal development

Continue to focus on the stage of the evolution process you are in and what's needed in order for you to grow. Then refer back to the 5 Principles of Mastery to figure out what you can do to further develop and improve these skills. Understanding where you are now, where you want to go and how you can get there, will see you grow by leaps and bounds. This is what I wish for you – for you to grow and develop to your full potential and become a thriving contributor in our industry.

Writing this book has been a labour of love. It's been an incredible experience looking back over my years of teaching and educating, to be able to bring my expertise to you in this book. To all of you who have reached this page of the book, I wish you every success in your career. Enjoy the journey and be proud of the impact you are making to hundreds and thousands of lives by *teaching dance beyond the steps*.

Author Q & A

Q | Usually – about once a year – generally when I'm starting back in the classroom after holidays, I start to question, 'Am I cut out for this? Can I still give my students what they need?' I've been teaching for years. I'm just wondering if you've ever felt like this?

A | Yes, absolutely! I call it a confidence crisis. The 'Who am I?' and 'Am I enough' self-talk. I think it's normal and quite healthy to revisit these questions from time to time. I find the best way to come back around, is to first go back and remember your 'why'. Why did you start dancing? Why did you want to teach? Why do you do what you do, and how does it make you feel? Asking these questions of yourself will reignite your passion, focus and motivation … and, if you are still struggling, simply ask someone who loves you why they think you're amazing!

Q | How can I get my students to feel comfortable talking to me, particularly in the beginning or when covering classes for another teacher?

A | I know that when you first walk into a classroom and you don't know the students it can feel a bit awkward. It's usually because there is complete silence. The secret is connection. Finding ways to connect and relate with each of the students in the class will put them at ease and then the atmosphere will begin to feel more relaxed.

Get on the same level as them (physically) and have a chat at the beginning of the lesson. Talk about your expectations of them, as well as letting them know how excited you are to be there to teach them. Try to add a little humour into the mix if you can, as once they crack a smile, they will start to relax and respect you.

Q | In the book, you talk about morning routines. What's your morning routine?

A | I'm not one of those people who wakes up really early. I wish I was but I find that I hit a wall about 2 pm if I'm up before 6 am. I set my alarm for 6.30 am and, as soon as I wake, I write in my journal and review my goals for the year. I write three things I'm grateful for and then three intentions I have for the day ahead. I then spend about 20 minutes meditating and calming my mind before the busyness of the day begins.

Once I'm done, I start the day with a green smoothie (home-grown greens from our green house), sort out my daughters for school and then I exercise. On a perfect day, I'm in the office by 9 am ready to start my day.

Q | Who inspires you?

A | Ohh ... this is a hard one, because there are so many people I admire! I'll talk about my top two.

I have to start with my husband. His motivation and drive across every area of his life is like none other I have seen. Every action is driven with his family in mind (me and our daughters) to give us the best life possible, which I am so thankful for.

Next is my mum, Sandra. She is the kindest, most generous person I know (and if you ask anyone who knows her, I'm sure they would agree with this). Her dedication and support for me, and our family, is beyond anything I could hope for. I would not be where I am today without her.

I try to be a combination of these two people every day.

Q | Are you planning on writing a sequel to this book?

A | Yes! I've already started to plan it out, in fact. My love for reading was only sparked about five years ago when I had a hunger to learn more and work on my personal development. Since then, I haven't stopped reading! It was through this time that I knew I wanted to share my message with others and publish my own book, even though I had no idea where to start.

I know many people read on electronic devices now, but I still love the feeling on holding a book in my hands and reading it from cover to cover.

About the Author

Jen Dalton's life philosophy is centred on empowering and educating dance teachers to be the best and most effective leaders they can be, and giving them the tools to make a positive impact in each and every life they come into contact with.

Having successfully owned and operated multiple dance studios for over 25 years – with over 1,000 students and managing teams of over 30 teachers and staff members at one time – Jen knows the importance of strategy, planning and being committed to continual learning.

By drawing on her many years of teaching dance and running her own studios, Jen can show you, too, how to streamline your dance studio operations or become the teacher that studio owners want to hire.

A well as teaching at and running her dance studios; Jen studied to be a police officer. She went on to work in the Child Protection and Sex Crimes Squad for 13 years. Jen studied Psychology and Communications at CSU, Health and Fitness, and Dance Teaching and Management. It was only natural that the next step was to collate all the information she learned from her studies and work experience to turn it into a dance industry manual, making it easy, quick and readily available for dancers and teachers around the world.

It is Jen's intention to create a worldwide community of like-minded dance teachers and educators who – together – will support, encourage and lead with the intention to fully equip our next generation of students for excellence. With her help and guidance, she hopes you will become the dance teacher you would have loved to be taught by.

Jen's training programs are designed in a way that make them easy to understand and, most importantly, easy to implement. Most dance teachers and dance studio owners undertake training in between running their classes each week. With this in mind, the dance teacher and studio owner training programs available through *Dance Teacher Central* have been designed to allow you to work at your own pace and pause for moments in order to implement some of the magic and get back to class.

Jen resides in Sydney, Australia with her incredibly supportive husband and two beautiful daughters.

For more information on Jen or *Dance Teacher Central*, please visit: www.danceteachercentral.com.

Jen Dalton | Speaker, Facilitator

Jen speaks on the topics of leadership, teaching, and personal and professional development. If you would like to book Jen, please email: info@danceteachercentral.com.

Acknowledgements

First and foremost, I would like to thank my fellow dance studio owners and teachers, who continue to support and encourage not only me, but also each other. It can be a lonely life in some ways, so to know that there are so many of you out there who are willing to take the time to give to one another, brings me joy and fills me with hope for our evolving industry.

I would like to specifically thank my own dance teacher, Miss Trish, who showed me that there is more to dance than the steps alone. Miss Trish, it was you who ignited the fire and passion within me to share my love for children, teaching and dance with as many people as possible.

To my amazing team of teachers who I have the privilege of working alongside each day, your enthusiasm, passion and dedication is infectious and I know how lucky I am to have you in my life. You make me proud every day. Wherever life takes you, I know that you will succeed.

Mum, I genuinely don't know how we would do life without you. I don't even have words to describe my love and gratitude for everything you do for my family and I. Don't even think about retiring and travelling the world!

Thank you to my girls, Mia and Isla. You had no choice but to start your life surrounded by this crazy and exciting world of dance, but you adapted to it beautifully and the way you conduct yourselves is far beyond your years. Both of you are capable, independent and kind to others. As your mum, I couldn't ask for anything more of you at this stage of your lives and I am proud to call you my daughters.

Finally, thank you to my husband, who continues to allow me to dream big and (although sometimes reluctantly) support me with every new idea I have, encouraging me to be the best version of myself. I know every decision you make and everything you do is to give me, and our girls, the best life possible. Thank you ... I love you.

Connect With Jen

Become part of the *Dance Teacher Central* community and join the other dance teachers to take these ideas to the next level. Connect with us here:

FACEBOOK: https://www.facebook.com/danceteachercentral/

INSTAGRAM: @danceteachercentral

Lightning Source UK Ltd.
Milton Keynes UK
UKHW020200110223
416808UK00010B/1395